the
inclusive
psalms

D1362133

the inclusive psalms

PRIESTS FOR EQUALITY
Brentwood, Maryland

PRIESTS FOR EQUALITY
P.O. Box 5243
W. Hyattsville, MD 20782-0243

Printed in the United States of America
99 98   5 4 3 2nd printing

Cover illustration by Melissa Cooper
Book designed by Craig R. Smith
Typeset in Book Antiqua and American Uncial

Library of Congress Catalog Card Number: 97-066497
ISBN 0-9644279-2-3

table of
contents

in memoriam

We dedicate this book to the memory
of Dr. Kenneth Jozwiak, our rhetorician, who died in an automobile
accident in the fall of 1996. Ken's gentle spirit and sensitivity had a
profound impact on the quality of our work. Ken, along with his partner,
Kate Barfield, exemplified the spirit of inclusivity and collaboration that
we are committed to bringing to everything we do. His depth of insight
and keen understanding of the nuances of the English language is appar-
ent to us on every page of this text. We are deeply saddened by the loss of
our friend and collaborator, and will always remember his contribution to
this work.

acknowledgments

In the fall of 1995, when we made the decision to publish *The Inclusive Psalms*, we were faced with a dilemma: the team that had worked together to produce *The Inclusive New Testament* had since dispersed. So we began this project with the faith that the perfect team would once again come together.

And so it did, *Deo gratias!* Each member of the team brought a plethora of gifts and talents, and each played an indispensable role in the production of *The Inclusive Psalms*. But beyond the considerable talents that each individual brought to the project, it is their commitment to inclusive language and their spirit of collaboration that made this book possible.

Many thanks, then, to the following people for their invaluable contribution to *The Inclusive Psalms*:

Barbara Marian (Feminist Theology, Liturgy) provided us with her expertise in liturgical reading. Her sensitivity to the sound and cadence of the spoken word helped us craft the text in a way that it can be easily read (and clearly understood) in public settings.

Mary Dougherty (Feminist Theology, Ecumenism) served as one of the readers of the texts. Her prayerful reading and struggles with *The Inclusive Psalms* gave us many practical insights into how the psalms apply to people in their daily lives.

Kate Barfield and Ken Jozwiak (Feminism, Rhetoric) once again demonstrated their skills and sensitivity to the nuances of language. Kate, an attorney, and Ken, a doctorate in English, worked as a team reading the texts aloud to each other, and both provided critical comments. Through their careful work and strong feminist sensibilities, they ensured that every line of the text was clear, understandable and compelling.

The Rev. Elizabeth Anderson (Pastoral Theology, Feminist Theology), the newest member of our team, provided keen insights and a careful editor's eye during the final stages of editing prior to publication.

Finally, I want to acknowledge the tireless work of our co-editors, **Mark Buckley** (Systematic Theology) **and Craig R. Smith** (Scripture), without whom the project could never have gone forward. Mark joined the team in the spring of 1996 as Technical Editor and theologian-in-residence. His creative crafting of the initial drafts, and continual review of the best new scripture scholarship, were immensely valuable. And Craig, our editor for *The Inclusive New Testament*, once again demonstrated his vast and diverse talents throughout every stage of the publication. He was responsible for the painstaking translation from the original Hebrew texts, and again did the design, layout and desktop publishing of the book.

Rev. Joseph A. Dearborn
National Secretary

introduction

following the success of our earlier work, *The Inclusive New Testament*, many have written to us to ask when we will produce "the rest of the Bible." Priests for Equality is now well on the way to completing that task. We plan to have completed our translation of the Hebrew Scriptures by July of the year 2000, our twenty-fifth anniversary. We'll publish it in three volumes, according to the traditional Jewish division: **the Law** (or *Torah*), **the Prophets** (or *Nevi'im*), and **the Writings** (or *Ketuvim*). This volume of *The Inclusive Psalms* is the first part of **the Writings**.

We are pleased to offer our new translation of the Psalms, which is being published separately for use in private and communal prayer and study.

The Book of Psalms

> Human beings write their lives word by word, line by line,
> with the thick dark ink of life, while at the same time God
> writes in between the lines with an ink as yet invisible.
>
> *Victor Hugo*

Sacred scripture is the Word of God in human words; it is a divine revelation, mediated through particular cultures and languages, and passed down through still other cultures and languages. It expresses the hopes and struggles of a people, their experience of the work of God in their lives. The book of Psalms is a part of this history: it expresses in song and poetry the life of a people who experienced themselves as a chosen people, with a special, divinely-appointed mission in the world. Their words search through the souls of their own time and culture as they labor to come to terms with this identity.

And through their writing, they reach through time to touch the lives of different peoples in different cultures—of us, who struggle to apply the Word of God in our lives.

℞ ℞ ℞

We all know the power of song to touch our hearts and inspire us. Imagine that one day you sit down, take up your guitar and begin to sing a song of spontaneous praise to God. You sing of your hopes, of your frustrations and times of despair, and your words strike a chord with your friends.

Then someone, moved and inspired by this spontaneous song, urges you to write down the words. Soon the song becomes part of the worship of your immediate circle of friends, then makes its way into your larger faith community. Someone else—adding directions to make it easier for large groups to perform your song—includes it in a hymnbook, and the song is widely disseminated. Then this book of hymns is combined with others to make a single larger hymnal.

Many years later, someone copies the lyrics into a book for spiritual reflection rather than song, your music having been lost along the way. And still later, scholars add numbers to the text so they can study it better, without being completely knowledgeable of the original musical directions. Then this text is translated into another language, which inevitably brings significant changes to the text—and to your song. This new translation soon becomes the preferred text, while the original one falls into disuse. This translated text is then used as the basis for other translations.

This is an oversimplification of how our modern translations of the Psalms came to be, but it gives you a feel for what happened. The book of Psalms is a collection of hymnbooks from ancient Israel. We've come a long way from the day when we ascribed the entire collection of 150 psalms to King David and left it at that. Scholars tell us that the sources for the psalms, the structure of the poems, and the ways they were originally used were all greatly diverse (with relatively few psalms attributable to David). Moreover, the process by which they came to be compiled into one book is quite complex, if not serendipitous. We know that certain psalms reflect certain periods in the history of Israel: some harken back to the court of David; others were earlier, dating back to the time when Judah and Israel were divided nations; still others are dated later, to the time of the Babylonian Exile and the post-exilic period.

An additional problem is the texts themselves. We have the standard Hebrew (Masoretic) texts, as well as the many variant readings from hundreds of ancient manuscripts. We also have the different Greek translations of Hebrew texts now lost to us—texts which were perhaps even more ancient than those which comprise the Masoretic text; the best-known such translation is the Septuagint, upon which the Latin Vulgate was based. It is not surprising, then, that in working with the great breadth of new scholarship, many new translators of the psalms, using the many different ancient versions available to us today, come to some varying—and sometimes contradictory—conclusions.

Our translation of the Psalms is no different. To develop our own translation, the editors of *The Inclusive Psalms* went painstakingly word by word through the Hebrew (and Greek translations of the Hebrew) texts. In the process of forming our inclusive text, we had to sift through numerous other translations, commentaries and lexicons to determine sometimes obscure meanings. And we also had to make some difficult choices along the way. At points, the meaning of the Hebrew text was obscure, and exhaustive research made it clear that every other translation had only given its best guess as to the meaning of the passage.

We say this not to scare you away from our translation, but rather to give you a broader understanding of the complex genesis of the book of Psalms, and by way of introduction to some of the reasons behind our editorial choices.

Translating songs and poetry from one language to another is a unique challenge. How to express the sentiments of one culture in another language is always perplexing. It becomes even more trying when you are dealing with ancient languages—Hebrew lyrics differ from English lyrics in just too many ways.

For instance, many forms of English poetry move from phrase to phrase in smooth and regular cadence, using balanced rhythms; Hebrew poetry, on the other hand, is often rough and terse, with each phrase tightly packed, frequently using parallel imagery and repetition to form its rhythm and meter. To English speakers, familiar with the soothing rhythms of standard English renditions of the Twenty-third Psalm, the original Hebrew can be very startling. In our translation, we tried to find a balance between the kind of poetic form familiar to the ears of the English-speaking public, and the earthy, gruff tone of the original language. At times we may have erred on one side or the other in our translation. In all cases, however, we have been guided by our commitment to produce the best inclusive language texts available.

೧ ೧ ೧

It is easy for Christians to read the Psalms from the perspective of the Christian scriptures, applying a form of interpretation known as typological hermeneutics, a method used in the early church. The typological interpretation of the Bible presents the people, institutions, or events of the Hebrew Scriptures as *symbols* which anticipate (and find their fulfillment in) the people, institutions or events of the Christian Scriptures. This method affirms a continuity between the two great scriptures, and ultimately the unity of God's saving activity in human history.

But as with any theological method, it is important to remember some very distinct differences. The Christian scriptures are permeated with the spirit of Jesus—every word always refers back to this individual and to the Christian confession of the uniqueness of Jesus in salvation history. The Hebrew scriptures, on the other hand, are permeated with the spirit of a people who saw themselves as having a distinctive mission among the nations, whose lives chronicle a constant struggle to determine how God was calling them to live out this mission.

Very often, Christians who use the Psalms as Christological hymns feel that parts of the Psalms don't seem consonant with the spirit of Jesus (or, indeed, with our modern pietistic sensibilities of what sacred scriptures *should* sound like). Worship services frequently edit out these "objectionable" parts.

For instance, one of the most striking elements of the book of Psalms is their strident militarist nationalism—their glorification of violence, and their supplications for God to wreak revenge on their enemies. God is often portrayed as a great warrior—the great protector of Israel who will give the foes of Israel a royal trouncing. And the psalmists provide us with all the gory details. Many people find such glorifications of violence disturbing, or have difficulty relating to God as a military leader. And equally disturbing, some have used these same passages to justify their own violence and oppression of others. Using religion to feed and excuse prejudice is not a new thing.

It must be remembered, however, that these songs reflect certain periods and stages in the history of Israel. The world of ancient Israel was a world of warrior tribes led by monarchs; one vision of the messiah was as such a warrior, someone who would conquer all the marauders from surrounding lands and protect the people. And people related to God with these images. Just as their own sovereign protected them and led them on to victory, so much more would God be their ultimate protector from hostilities of the surrounding world.

That being said, in some ways our world is not that different from the world of ancient Israel. We are still surrounded by violence—by wars and rumors of war—on our streets, among our cultures, and between nations. We still have to deal with corrupt political institutions and duplicitous leaders. Disease and hardship still threaten our lives and the lives of those we love, even down through several generations. Ethnic, tribal and gender differences still divide us, and fuel further violence in reaction to the damage they cause. Violence begets violence in our cities and in our homes, and through the media we are all witnesses to the violence and oppression of people throughout the world. Violence fills our music, from the explicit lyrics and incessant beat of Rap to the seemingly benign militarism of a Sousa march or a national anthem. We still pray for God's protection from oppression—from sexism and racism, or from random urban violence—often oblivious to the ways in which we ourselves perpetuate or tacitly accept these very things through our media and culture. And we still hope, perhaps in secret, that those who oppress us will get what's coming to them. If ancient Israelites could not see beyond their own ethnic and tribal biases, we cannot judge them too harshly—for we too are often unaware of our own biases.

The psalms express the hope for deliverance from the things that lurk in the shadows—shadows without and within. Human beings have changed very little from ancient times: we all have a shadow side in need of redemption. The "thick, dark ink" which the psalmists write with comes from their own experiences—their hopes and dreams, their fears and times of despair, their imperfect demands to God for justice and for protection. Their words still speak to us and put us in touch with the fullness of our humanity before God, bumps, warts, bruises and all—and God is still writing in between the lines with an ink as yet invisible.

Many of those who reviewed the initial drafts of our translations had a difficult time with the martial tenor of the Psalms, and we struggled quite a bit with it too in our own work with the texts. We made a very conscious editorial decision not to significantly soft-pedal it. To do so would have meant actually removing some major parts of the text, or re-writing them to such a degree that it would no longer be what the psalmist said. We wanted to psalmists to speak for themselves, and to speak to a part of us that we sometimes don't want to admit.

Beyond that, our editorial choices are governed by the guidelines that we have developed over the years to present the Scriptures in a non-sexist and a non-classist manner.

Guiding Principles

In our work with inclusive language, we have developed a set of guiding principles which we have applied to all of our work. These guiding principles can be stated as follows:

❖ **To create a "critical feminist biblical interpretation" of sacred scripture that is inclusive in both content and process.**

From the beginning of the project, our efforts have involved grassroots feedback, the guidance of feminist theology and scripture scholarship, and an editorial process that includes women and men skilled in both the theological and social aspects of feminist, pastoral and scriptural critique.

❖ **To present the text in a layout that enhances the flow of the text, emphasizing the particular literary form that the text uses, while retaining the traditional chapters and verses.**

The modern divisions of the books of the Bible into chapters most likely happened in the 13th century; separating the text into numbered verses occurred in the 16th century. The verses of the psalms were originally numbered by religious scholars long after the psalms were used by singers, choirs and congregations in public worship. Taken as they were out of their musical context, many of the directions for musical accompaniment, and other comments added to elucidate their musical origin, were incorporated by these scholars into the text of the psalms themselves. Moroever, the verse numberings vary greatly from one source to the next; our version places the introductory material of a psalm outside the regular verse numbering. We have also attempted to make the poetry of the psalms as evident as possible from the page design.

❖ **To make a clear distinction between linguistic convention and overt bias in passages that appear sexist, and to distinguish between those passages which simply exclude women and those which actively vilify women.**

The most difficult problem we have had to address is what can be done with the sexism in scripture without destroying the actual text. Several guiding principles have emerged from our work on this problem. One principle has been to determine whether the text uses a linguistic convention that seems sexist to our modern sensibilities, or whether the underlying meaning of the text itself is inherently sexist. In all circumstances, we seek to recover the original meaning of the text without perpetuating the sexist or classist idioms. To do this, we have employed some of the most current biblical scholarship and feminist critique available today.

❖ **To use terminology that acknowledges the many forms in which God appears in our lives.**

The most common names of God used in the Psalms are *Elohim* and *Yahweh*. The Hebrew word *Elohim* is a plural noun that is used to designate a single entity. The cognate *El* is masculine, while the plural ending is feminine—so *Elohim* actually balances the feminine and masculine elements of God. This is difficult to translate into English, so we have been careful to avoid pronouns of either gender when referring to God.

The name *Yahweh* presents us with other problems. Following the ancient Jewish practice of not speaking or writing the tetragrammaton YHWH, the Hebrew term *Adonai,* or "Lord," has been traditionally substituted. In many standard translations, the word "LORD" (completely uppercased) is used to translate *Yahweh*, and "Lord" (not uppercased) to translate *Adonai*. However, we do not use the English word "Lord" in our translations because of its sexist and classist connotations.

Our approach is to follow traditional Jewish practice and use "Adonai" when *Yahweh* is being used as a form of address. In fact, we frequently take psalms that refer to Yahweh in the third person and recast them in the first and second person, so that God is talked *with* and not just *about*, an insight from Matin Buber's groundbreaking work ***I and Thou***. However, when the text speaks about Yahweh in the third person, we substitute the phrases "Our God" or "Your God" (with *Our* and *Your* always capitalized) to stress the covenantal relationship with God.

To avoid confusion, where the Hebrew word *adonai* occurs in the original text, we actually translate the term as "sovereign" or "Sovereign One," particularly when God's rulership is being described.

While we have taken great pains to use non-gender-specific language, most personal references in common speech employ gender-specific pronouns—necessarily so and, for the most part, inoffensively. In the case of the Psalms, we made our choices as the occasion warranted.

❖ To restore the role of women and of feminine images of God in scripture.

The role of women, and of female images of God, in the history of salvation has become obscured by centuries of sexism. Guided by recent feminist scholarship, we have attempted to recover both the role of women in the history of salvation and the feminine images that are used of God. The God of the psalmists is not merely the warrior and protector, but is also nurturing and caring.

At other times, our word choices hide a great deal of wrestling with the translation. A case in point is one of the names for God, *El Shaddai*. Many translators will render this as "God of the Mountains," referring, presumably, to Mt. Horeb and Mt. Zion. But many feminist scholars have pointed out that the root word of *Shaddai* is "breast"—and that a more accurate rendition of *El Shaddai* might be "the Breasted God," an obviously feminine image. Unfortunately, the two places where *Shaddai* appears in the Psalms are rife with overtly masculine imagery, and using "the Breasted One" in those contexts would simply be too jarring, so we have left the word untranslated.

❖ To maintain a preferential option for those relegated to society's margins.

It is becoming fairly standard practice to avoid characterizing people by a particular accident of birth or fortune. The Word of God invites everyone in, and God does not judge people by externals. Our goal throughout has been to humanize individuals and declare God's preferential option for those at the margins of society. To that end we strive to acknowledge the dignity of each individual by the simple expedient of how we address them.

In our choice of words to describe enemies, our choices are appropriate to our time: where most translations speak of deliverance from "the wicked," we actually speak of deliverance from "those who commit violence" or from "corrupt individuals." The word "wicked" has taken on a meaning in our own culture that is almost the opposite of what it used to mean: when many youth speak of something as "wicked," they mean that it is intense; in certain colloquial New England parlance, a "wicked good chowder" is especially flavorful. This does not really get to the heart of what the psalmists are saying. In Hebrew, those who are described as wicked are often those who perform acts of violence; and those who are evil are committing crimes or are politically corrupt. In many cases, the term used refers to some very concrete types of behavior. These terms lose their power when they are turned into abstractions. Too often the terms "evil" and "wicked" are abstractions that remove us far from the life experience of the psalmist, and indeed from our own life experience. We believe that, in most cases, our word choices are more faithful to the meaning of the Hebrew as well as to our own experience.

❖ **To stress the mutuality and equality of human relationships**.

Given that many of these texts were written for the Royal Court, it is understandable that they would have many references to "kings" and "servants." Such references, read today, reflect the sexism and classism of their times. For "kings" or "princes" we have used "leaders" or "rulers" or, occasionally, "those who hold power." In very few cases, such as the Royal Wedding psalm, the gender specific references were so specific that it would have been impossible to render the psalm into completely inclusive language.

It also reflected the classism of that time to have slaves and servants— and this metaphor is extended to denote a special relationship to God. Indeed, David is called God's servant. While it may be easy for us to understand the use of the term "servant" or to dismiss the use of the term "slave" as a mere historical reference, we do so at the risk of losing sight of our own classism or of the ways we are blind to the inequalities in our world. Recognizing the historical reality of servants and slaves, we have chosen to emphasize function rather than social status. Thus, for "servant" we have used "attendant" when the text refers to service toward another human being. In relation to God, however, such as "servant of God," we generally use the word "faithful one."

While it is historically the case that, during at least part of the time that the psalms were written, the people of Israel relied on their (male) ruler to give them a sense of communal identity, it is the special relationship of the ruler to God that must be emphasized. Kings were anointed just as prophets were anointed—and they rose or fell according to their faithfulness to God. It's easy to speak of "kings" or "kingdoms," but what lies behind them is a communal sense of identity. So instead of "kingdom" we generally use "people" or "nation" when the word refers to a group identity. When the word refers to a particular geographic region or the reach of authority of a particular ruler, we use "realm" or "reign."

One other usage in this translation deserves special attention. We capitalize the terms "Anointed One" and "Chosen One" when they refer specifically to David or are used as a prefigurement of the Messiah. Otherwise, we lowercase them as a way of indicating that God's anointing is not restricted to a prophet or head of state—that women and men everywhere become "anointed ones" when they hear God's call to ministry and experience the Spirit's empowering presence.

A Note on "Selah"

We want to highlight a word that appears periodically throughout our translation of the Psalms, the rather cryptic word *selah*. A verb literally meaning to "lift up" (as in voices) or "exalt," *selah* was, according to *The New Brown-Driver-Briggs-Gesenius Hebrew and English Lexicon* (1978), used in early Jewish prayer books by at least 100 C.E., in the Benedictions; Jerome classes *selah* with *amen* and *shalom*, and Jacob of Edessa compares it with the Christian "Amen" of the people after the Gloria. *Selah* is clearly associated with music, and "probably came into use in the late Persian period in connection with psalms used with musical accompaniment in public worship, to indicate [the] place of benedictions."

Our translators have come to believe that *selah*, which almost always appears at emotional high points in the psalms, denoted a pause in the singing during which the congregation was invited to freely add their own praises, blessings, or heartfelt interjections, as is done today in the worship services of a number of Christian traditions. Were we to translate the word, we would render it as "the congregation responds freely"—a direction to those assembled to "lift up" their voices in reply to the psalmist's words.

It should be noted, however, that the meaning of *selah* is hotly debated. Some scholars believe *selah* meant a musical interlude, or a pause in the music altogether; others believe it denoted a crescendo in the music, or even a diminuendo (though this latter doesn't seem terribly likely given the contexts in which *selah* appears). Because of this controversy, and out of a fear that some of our readers may find a translation of *selah* too disruptive to the flow of the poetry, we have followed the lead of most modern versions and haven't translated *selah* at all.

However, we suggest you try an experiment in your worship communities: Have some of you sing or pray the psalms, perhaps with a musical accompaniment, and have others only listen, and see if the places where *selah* appears don't lend themselves to spontaneous emotional response— words of praise, or prayer, or even outbursts of anger or frustration or supplication—by the listeners. Many of our worship services would do well to inject some well-ordered spontaneity into their litugical life!

Conclusion

What we have attempted here is to remove some of the layers of our own cultural impediments—baggage that we have carried for much too long—and reach back into history to hear the ancient echos of the music of the psalmists. In all cases, we have attempted to draw clear distinctions between the sexism and classism that infects our own lives and the historical contexts in which the psalmists were writing. And we have at all times attempted to be faithful to the words and the spirit of the original.

Sexism—like racism, ageism and any other form of bias—permeates our language and culture on many different levels. Sometimes these things are rather obvious and easily challenged; other times it is not so obvious. We can find a good example of this in the Civil Rights movement. It was obvious to many Americans that racism existed in the South: Jim Crow laws and ballot box laws attempted to keep African Americans from exercising their civil rights, while the local police and the Klan (often times the same people) enforced a reign of terror. When sympathizers came down from the North on Freedom Rides to stand against the forces of racism, it appeared that the United States was polarized once again between North and South. Yet Martin Luther King once commented that he had never experienced racism in the South to the degree that he experienced it in Chicago. Racism permeated the North as much as the South, but in far more subtle ways—and it didn't take much to make the undercurrent of racism in the North become patently manifest. Riots over the issue of busing in Boston and other northern cities left little doubt that racism permeated the whole country.

The psalms are part of the prayer and worship of two great religious traditions. They have been in use in synagogues and churches for centuries, chanted by cantors and monks and read by faithful all over the world. People turn to the psalms to hear the Liberating Word, Yet, when that word is covered over by centuries of sexist attitudes and prejudices, it is often very difficult to hear what God is really saying. Like layers of soot covering an ancient mosaic, sexism covers over the liberating word of God, hiding its true beauty and turning people away.

Our work in translating *The Inclusive Psalms* has been humbling, for we have had to face our own humanity, our own imperfections, and our own limitations along the way. The way *through* biases and oppressive attitudes is to face them head on—whether they are found in society or in ourselves—and to recognize them for what they are. The psalms force us to be honest with ourselves before God and to look to God for liberation from those things that still bind us. These are hymns of praise to God from ancient times and for our times.

We do not claim that the translation we present here is the final word about the book of Psalms—to do such would be the sin of hubris. We do believe, however, that this translation is a faithful rendition of the words of the psalmists in contemporary, inclusive English. Our hope is that our readers will find these words freeing and inspiring, and through these words, will hear the still, small voice of God in their lives.

Some Background for New Friends

Priests for Equality's Inclusive Language Project

Priests for Equality is a movement of women and men throughout the world—laity, religious and clergy—who work for the full participation of women and men in the church and in society. We are a grassroots organization committed to creating a culture where sexism and exclusion are behind us, and equality and full participation are the order of the day. We challenge sexism in all its forms wherever we may find it, and offer an alternative vision that frees and empowers people. One of the founding goals of Priests for Equality is to eliminate sexist language. This has been a prime focus for us through our **Inclusive Language Project.**

The project began in 1988, when Priests for Equality received permission to use inclusive language texts developed by Dignity, San Francisco. We distributed them to our constituency; their feedback spurred us to revise the texts significantly—revisions that reflected their actual use in the very settings they were being used: college campuses, parishes, chapels, houses of formation, convents, religious communities and living rooms.

In a formal follow-up survey, with close to three hundred responses, our users reported back—emphatically and with near-unanimity—that their priority in lectionary revision was "God-language." About this time, the National Conference of Catholic Bishops—who were undertaking to revise the Catholic Lectionary—explicitly voted not to change the masculine God-language. Yet in the draft of a pastoral letter on women's concerns, the bishops had already named sexism as a sin.

Our audience reacted swiftly and vocally. It quickly became clear that we—the rank and file of the church, feminists, feminist-oriented priests, and Priests for Equality—must now assume the responsibility for the creation of an inclusive lectionary. The bishops' decision confirmed what most of the Inclusive Language Project participants had suspected all along: if change were to come, it had to be from the people in the parishes and communities. A new readiness to implement inclusive language at the local level took hold, and there was a new energy at all levels to make inclusive language the issue of the '90s.

Priests for Equality went on to create a two-volume set of daily lectionary readings, and again revised its three-year Sunday lectionaries, to much acclaim. But the demand for an inclusive language version of the complete New Testament began to grow, and we happily undertook the project. In all, *The Inclusive New Testament* took seven years and the work of many dedicated individuals to complete, and was published in 1994.

The Power of Language

Language is the most significant tool for creating and reshaping society's perceptions—whether for good or for evil. Language shapes our perceptions. Language is praxis; it has the power to abuse or to heal. According to the 8th Day Center for Justice,

> Power and domination are intrinsic to language, which becomes a map of our social relationships—of the way we have granted power and authority to some and impotence and subjugation to others.

Yet language does more than reflect the society: it is also the primary instrument for effecting changes in the power structure. It has the power to change minds. It stirs people to action. It is nothing short of revolutionary.

From the day we were founded, we have dedicated ourselves to the elimination of sexist language and stereotyped roles from church worship, liturgical texts and from the scriptures. It's there in our charter: "We affirm efforts to use sexually balanced language and images in Church liturgy, publications, education and preaching."

Language—seemingly innocuous and inconsequential—is in reality an area which reveals unconscious attitudes and prejudices, stereotyopes, and patterns of discriminatroy thinking. The English usage of male pronouns for God and for human beings in general is a good example of this. We used to speak of "the brotherhood of man," not thinking that we were excluding over half the human race. Yet implied in our language was the presuppoison that the male was the standard of the human.

Conversely, care in language is a first and necessary step in raising consciousness. It can, in itself, help push us forward equally. In our work, we seek to bring about a transformation in our present day religious language and the way that we translate and interpret the sacred scriptures through that language. Our goal is not to change scripture, but rather to change the way we think about scripture. We seek to free the language of scripture from the "culture of sexism" into which it was translated in a way that the message of equality can be heard. We seek to recover in the ancient texts the stories of *both* women and men who struggled with their faith, who were faithful to their vision. To this end, we consciously adopt an emancipatory religious rhetoric to recover our hidden history in a way that opens up the texts so that women and men today can listen to the ancient stories and actually experience themselves as included in the history of salvation. We believe that the sacred scriptures are inclusive words of Life.

Creation of the Text

Our inclusive scripture work—and *The Inclusive Psalms* is a case in point—is essentially a four-phase process.

We start by creating a working document. We begin with the raw text, then edit it according to a carefully-crafted style sheet we have developed, meticulously reworking sexist, classist and racist language.

Then the texts are reviewed by an independent scriptural scholar who is responsible for carefully editing them, working from the best ancient manuscripts in the original languages, and using cutting-edge biblical research as a critical tool.

The texts are then given to the Technical Committee, which also works through the text line by line. Our Technical Committee, which serves as an editorial board, represents four disciplines: Scripture, Feminism and Feminist Theology, Systematic Theology, and Pastoral Theology. The committee is small by design—three to five people at any one time—with a number of different individuals representing the four disciplines, and, on occasion, one individual representing more than one discipline. Throughout the process of creating our inclusive language versions, the Technical Committee remains a constant critical entity. This arrangement also allows us to use various consultants during the process, while assuring continuity throughout.

Outside consultants handle the desktop publishing, copy editing and proofreading. The important last step is a fresh and independent reading of the final draft by each member of the Technical Committee, after which the Committee meets and, in consultation with the scriptural scholar, comes to consensus on the final version, which then goes on to publication.

1   Happiness comes to those
        who reject the path of violence,
    who refuse to associate with criminals
        or even to sit with people who belittle others.
2   Happiness comes to those
        who delight in the Law of Our God
        and meditate on it day and night.
3   They're like trees planted by flowing water—
        they bear fruit in every season,
    and their leaves never wither:
        everything they do will prosper.

4   But not wrongdoers!
        They're like chaff that the wind blows away.
5   They won't have a taproot to anchor them
        when judgment comes,
    nor will corrupt individuals be given a place
        at the gathering of the Just.

6   Our God watches over the steps
        of those who do justice;
    but those on a path of violence and injustice
        will find themselves irretrievably lost.

1 Why are the nations creating such an uproar?
Why all this commotion among the peoples?
2 Those who hold power
are taking their stand,
gathering their forces against Our God,
against God's Anointed One.
3 "Let's break their chains!" they say.
"Let's throw off their shackles!"

4 But the One who sits enthroned in the heavens laughs;
the Sovereign One derides them,
5 then rebukes them in anger
and, enraged, terrifies them:
6 "It is I who installed my ruler on Zion,
on the mountain of my holiness!"

7 I will proclaim God's decree—
Our God said to me:
"You are my own;
I've given birth to you today.
8 Just ask—I'll give you the nations as your inheritance!
I'll give you the ends of the earth as your possession!
9 You'll break them with an iron scepter;
you'll shatter them as easily as a clay pot."

10 So, you rulers, be wise!
And you who hold power, stand warned!
11 Serve Our God and rejoice—
but do so with fear and trembling.
12 Pay homage to God's Own
lest you be destroyed on your way in a blaze of anger—
for God's passion can flare up without warning.

Happiness comes to those
who make God their refuge!

3

A psalm of David
Written when he fled from his son Absalom

1 O God, so many people have turned against me!
    So many are in open rebellion!
2 More and more are telling me,
    "No deliverance is coming to you from your God!"
        —— *Selah* ——

3 But you, Adonai, are my protection, my glory,
    the One who helps me hold up my head.
4 I cry aloud to you, Adonai,
    and you answer me from the mountain of your holiness.
        —— *Selah* ——
5 Now I can lie down and sleep, and then awake again,
    for you have hold of me—
6 no fear now of those tens of thousands
    who stand against me wherever I turn.

7 Arise, Adonai!
    Save me, my God!
You struck all my enemies with a blow to the jaw,
    and broke the teeth of the violent.

8 From you, Adonai—deliverance;
    to your people—blessing.

4

To the conductor: for strings
A psalm of David

1 Answer me when I call, God of my justice!
    Give me relief from my distress!
2 Have mercy!
    Hear my prayer!

How long will you people dishonor me before God?
    How long will you love delusion and pursue lies?
        —— *Selah* ——
3 Know that those who love Our God
    have been set apart by divine will—
    Our God will hear me when I call!
4 Tremble, and stop your sinning;
    search your heart,
    alone and silent in your room.
5 Offer sacrifices of justice,
    and put your trust in Our God.

6 So many are asking,
    "Does good even exist anymore?"
Let the light of your face, Adonai,
    shine on us!
7 You put joy in my heart—
    a joy greater than being full
    of bread and new wine.
8 In peace I'll lie down,
    in peace I will sleep:
for you alone, Adonai,
    keep me perfectly safe.

To the conductor: for wind instruments
A psalm of David

1 Take note of my words, Adonai!
　　Understand my sighs!
2 Listen to my cry for help, my Ruler, my God—
　　for it is to you that I pray.
3 Adonai, every morning you hear my voice,
　　every morning I put my requests before you, and I wait.

4 You're not a God who delights in treachery—
　　evil cannot live with you.
5 Arrogant people cannot stand in your presence;
　　you hate all who twist the truth;
6 you destroy those who lie,
　　and abhor the bloodthirsty and deceitful.

7 But I, because of your great love,
　　will enter your House;
　I will worship in your holy Temple
　　in awe and reverence.
8 Because of my enemies, guide me in your justice;
　　make straight your way before me.

9 For nothing they say can be trusted:
　　their hearts teem with treacheries,
　their throats are open graves,
　　and their tongues speak nothing but deceit.
10 Pronounce sentence on them, O God!
　　Let them fall by their own devices!
　Because they fall away from your word, banish them,
　　for they've been in open rebellion against you.

11 But let all who take refuge in you
　　be glad and rejoice forever.
　Protect them,
　　so that those who love your Name
　　will rejoice in you.
12 As for the just, Adonai,
　　you surround them with the shield of your will.

To the conductor: for strings, tuned an octave higher
A psalm of David

1   Adonai, don't rebuke me in your anger,
        don't chastise me in your wrath.
2   Have mercy on me, Adonai,
        for my strength is gone.
     Heal me,
        for I am afraid to my very bones,
3   and my soul is full of anguish.

     And you, Adonai—how long?
4   Turn, Adonai! Save my life!
        Deliver me because of your love.
5   For in death no one remembers you.
        Who can give you praise from the tomb?
6   I am exhausted from crying;
        every night I flood my bed with tears,
        I drench my couch with my weeping.
7   I'm nearly blind with grief;
        my eyes are weak because of all my foes.

8   Get away from me, all you who incite to violence,
        for Adonai has heard the sound of my weeping.
9   Adonai has heard my supplication
        and accepts my prayer.
10   May all my enemies be ashamed and panic-stricken!
        May they turn back in sudden disgrace!

*A frenzied musical rant, which David sang to Our God
about Cush, of the tribe of Benjamin*

1 Adonai, my God, I take refuge in you.
    Save me from those who hound me!
2 Rescue me, or my enemies will tear me to pieces like a lion
    and rip me to shreds, with no one to save me.

3 O God, if my hands have done wrong,
4   if I have done evil to someone who was at peace with me,
    or was dishonest even with my enemy,
5 then let my foe pursue and overtake me
    and trample my life to the ground!
    Let my honor sleep in the dust!
            —— *Selah* ——

6 Wake up, Adonai!
    Rise up in your anger
    against the fury of my enemies!
    Awake, my God,
    and give me justice!
7 Let the company of nations gather around you,
    and rule over them from on high.
8 Let Our God judge the peoples fairly—
    and judge me fairly as well, Most High!
    Prove my innocence and integrity!

9 Put an end to the violence all around me!
    Make the just feel secure, O God of justice,
    you who test mind and heart!
10 You are my shield, God Most High,
    who saves the upright of heart.

11 God, you are a just judge,
    a God whose anger would blaze forth every day
12   if you were not so forgiving!
    Even so, you sharpen your sword
    and bend and string your bow.
13 You have prepared your deadly weapons
    and readied your flaming arrows.

14 Those who are full of malice and conceive evil
　　bring forth nothing but disillusionment.
15 Those who dig deep pitfalls for others
　　will fall into their own traps.
16 Their malice recoils right back on them,
　　and their violence will fall on their own head.

17 I thank Our God for being so just!
　　I sing praise to the Name of Adonai Most High!

8

To the conductor: to be played on the Gittite harp
A psalm of David

1 Adonai, Our God, how majestic is your Name in all the earth!
　　You have placed your glory above the heavens!
2 From the lips of infants and children
　　you bring forth words of power and praise,
to answer your adversaries
　　and to silence the hostile and vengeful.

3 When I behold your heavens, the work of your fingers,
　　the moon and the stars which you have set in place—
4 what is humanity that you should be mindful of us?
　　Who are we that you should care for us?
5 You have made us barely less than God,
　　and crowned us with glory and honor.
6 You have made us responsible
　　for the works of your hands,
　　putting all things at our feet—
7 all sheep and oxen,
　　yes, even the beasts of the field,
8 the birds of the air, the fish of the sea
　　and whatever swims the paths of the seas.

9 Adonai, Our God,
　　how majestic is your Name in all the earth!

1 I will praise you, Adonai, with my whole heart;
      I will tell of all your marvelous works!
2 I will be glad and rejoice in you,
      I will sing praise to your Name, Most High!

3 When my enemies are turned back,
      they stumble and are lost in your presence.
4 For you have maintained my right and my cause;
      you occupy the judgment seat, a righteous judge.
5 You have rebuked the nations, and destroyed the violent.
      You blotted out their name forever and ever.
6 The enemy has been cut down;
      their ruins are endless.
   You have overthrown their cities,
      and even the memory of them has vanished.

7 But you, Adonai, reign forever
      and have established your throne of judgment.
8 You will judge the world in justice
      and govern the peoples with equity.
9 For you, Adonai, are a refuge for the oppressed,
      a stronghold in times of trouble.
10 Those who know your Name trust in you,
      for you have never forsaken those who seek you, Adonai.

11 Sing praise to Our God enthroned in Zion,
      declare God's work among the nations!
12 For the One who avenges blood remembers them,
      and doesn't ignore the cry of the afflicted.

13 Have mercy on me, Adonai!
      See what I suffer from those who hate me!
   Lift me up from the gates of death,
14   that I may recount all your praises—

---

* Psalms 9 and 10 were originally a single poem. Together they form an acrostic poem: the first
letter of each stanza begins with a subsequent letter of the Hebrew alphabet.

that in the gates of the Daughter of Zion
   I may rejoice in your deliverance!
15   The nations have fallen into the pit they dug,
   the net they set caught their own feet.
16   In passing sentence, you are manifest;
   you are known, Adonai, for your just judgments:
the violent are trapped
   by the work of their own hands.
          —— *Selah; meditation* ——

17   Sheol will become the home of the godless—
   all those who forget Our God.
18   But the needy will not always be forgotten,
   the hope of the poor will not be lost forever.

19   Arise, Adonai! Don't let them be victorious!
   Let the nations be judged in your presence!
20   Strike them with terror, Adonai,
   and let the nations know that they are only human.
          —— *Selah* ——

10·1 Why do you stand aloof, Adonai?
   Why do you seem to hide yourself in times of trouble?
2   The violent arrogantly pursue the weak
   and catch them in craftily designed schemes.
3   The impious boast of the desires of their hearts;
   they bless Greed, yet renounce you, Adonai.
4   With their noses in the air they never seek you;
   they think and say, "There is no God!"
5   Though their ways always prosper,
   your judgments are on high, out of their sight;
haughtily they keep your laws far away from themselves,
   and they sneer at all their enemies.
6   They think in their hearts, "We will not be moved;
   throughout all generations, we'll be happy and untroubled."
7   Their mouths are filled with cursing and deceit and oppression;
   under their tongues are mischief and iniquity.
8   They sit in ambush in the villages;
   they ambush the innocent and murder them;
   they stalk their victims in secret.

9   They lie in wait like a lion in the bushes;
        they lie in wait to catch the helpless:
        they catch the poor by drawing them into their net.
10 Their victims are crushed,
        they collapse and fall under their oppressors' strength.
11 But the violent only say, "God has forgotten,"
        or, "God is looking the other way and will never see this."

12 Wake up, Adonai! O God, lift up your hand!
        Don't forget those who are helpless!
13 Why do the violent renounce you, God?
        Why do they say in their hearts,
        "You won't call me to account"?
14 But you *do* see;
        you see every trouble, every cause for grief;
        you ponder it and take it into your hand.
    The helpless commit themselves to you;
        you are the helper of the orphan.
15 Break the arm of the violent and the evildoer!
        Seek out corruption till you find no more!

16 You will rule forever and ever, Adonai,
        and those who don't acknowledge you
        will perish from the land.
17 Adonai, you hear the desire of the meek;
        you strengthen their hearts
        and bend your ear to them,
18 to do justice to the orphan and the oppressed
        so that those born of earth may strike terror no more.

11

1   I take refuge in Our God,
        yet this is what I hear from everyone:
    "Bird, fly back to your mountain refuge and hide!"
2   Or: "See how the violent are bending their bows
        and fitting their arrows to the string,
        ready to ambush the innocent from the shadows!"
3   Or: "When the foundations are being destroyed,
        what can an honest person do?"

4   But I say:
    Our God is in the holy Temple,
        Our God rules from heaven!
    The eyes of God see all,
        and examine the human condition.
5   Our God watches over the just,
        but stands against the oppressor and those who love violence,
6   raining down fire and brimstone on the ruthless;
        a scorching wind is all they'll get to eat or drink.
7   For Our God is just, and loves justice—
        the upright will see God's face.

12

1   Help, Adonai! No one is loving any more;
        faithfulness has vanished from the peoples.
2   Neighbor lies to neighbor;
        their words are smooth and duplicitous.
3   May Our God destroy all smooth talkers,
        every boastful tongue, and those who say,

4   "We can talk our way out of anything!
     We know *just* how to twist our words,
     so that no one can challenge us."

5   "Because they oppress the helpless,
     because poor people sigh and moan,
     now I will rise up!" says Our God.
6   The promises of Our God are flawless,
     like refined silver, freed from dross, purified seven times over.
7   You, Adonai, will keep us safe and protect us always
     from this generation—
8   where corrupt people strut proudly around,
     and the scum of the earth hold high office.

13

For the conductor
A psalm of David

1   How long, Adonai? Will you forget me forever?
     How long will you hide your face from me?
2   How long must I wrestle with my anguish,
     and wallow in despair all day long?
     How long will my enemy win over me?

3   Look at me! Answer me, Adonai, my God!
     Give light to my eyes, lest I sleep the sleep of death,
4   lest my enemy say, "I have prevailed,"
     lest my foes rejoice when I fall.

5   I trust in your love;
     my heart rejoices in the deliverance you bring.
6   I'll sing to you, Adonai,
     for being so good to me.

14

For the conductor
By David

1 Only fools say to themselves.
     "There is no God!"
   They're all corrupt,
       they've done terrible things,
       and no one does what is right.
2 Our God looks down from heaven upon the peoples
       to see if anyone understands,
       if anyone seeks God.
3 But they are all lost,
       they are all equally corrupt;
   not one of them does what is right,
       not a single one.
4 Will they never learn?
   They eat up my people like bread
       and never give God a thought.
5 I see them now, consumed with fear,
       because God is on the side of those who do justice.
6 They frustrate the progress of poor people at every turn,
       but Our God is the refuge of those in need.

7 Who will God bring us from Zion?
       Who will be the Deliverance of Israel?
   When Our God makes the faithful prosperous again,
       what joy and celebration will be ours
       as children of Leah and Rachel and Jacob!

By David

1 Who has the right to enter your tent, Adonai,
        or to live on your holy mountain?
2 Those who conduct themselves with integrity,
        and work for justice;
   who speak the truth from their heart,
3   and do not use their tongues for slander;
   who do not wrong their neighbors,
        and cast no discredit on their friends;
4 who look with contempt on the corrupt,
        but honor those who revere Our God;
   who always keep their promises
        even when it hurts;
5 who don't demand interest on loans,
        and cannot be bribed to exploit the innocent.

   If people do these things,
        nothing can ever shake them.

A poem of David

1   O God, keep me safe—
      you are my refuge!
2   I said to Our God, "You are my God;
      there is nothing good for me apart from you."

3   The holy people of my land are wonderful!
      My greatest pleasure is to be with them.
4   But those who rush after other gods
      will bring many troubles upon themselves.
    I will not take part in their sacrifices;
      I won't even speak the names of their gods.

5   You, Adonai, are all that I have,
      you are my food and drink.
      My life is safe in your hands.
6   Within the boundaries you set for me
      there are nothing but pleasant places!
      What a delightful inheritance I have!

7   I praise Our God, who guides me;
      even at night my heart teaches me.
8   I'm always aware of your presence;
      you are right by my side, and nothing can shake me.
9   My heart is happy and my tongue sings for joy;
      I feel completely safe with you,
10 because you won't abandon me to the Grave;
      you won't let your loved one see decay.
11 You show me the path to Life;
      your presence fills me with joy,
      and by your side I find enduring pleasure.

A prayer of David

1 Adonai, I plead for a just cause!
    Listen to my cry!
  Turn your ear to my prayer,
    for my lips are free from untruth.
2 Prove my integrity—
    let your eyes see what is true!
3 You search my heart,
    you visit me by night.
  You test me and find nothing wrong:
    I determined that my mouth wouldn't sin!
4 And as for my actions,
    because of the word you spoke to me,
  I was able to avoid a path
    that leads to violence.
5 I kept my feet firmly on your road,
    and my steps never faltered.

6 Now I am the one calling to you—
    and you, O God, will answer me.
  Turn your ear to me
    and hear my prayer.
7 Show me your steadfast love—
    and your great strength.
  Save those who take refuge in you
      from those who hate them.
8 Guard me as the apple of your eye;
    hide me in the shadow of your wings,
9 and from violent and ruthless attacks—
    from my enemies who surround me with deadly intent.
10 They close their hearts to compassion,
    but open their mouths in arrogance.
11 They've tracked me down;
    now they surround me.
   Their eyes are alert,
    ready to strike me to the ground
12 as though they were hungry lions about to pounce
    or a young lion crouched in the bushes.

¹³ Adonai, arise! Confront them, strike them down!
    Rescue me from the violent with your sword!
¹⁴ Let your hand rescue me from such people,
    from such a world,
    from people whose only reward is in this present life.

You fill the bellies of those you cherish;
    their children will have plenty,
    and will store up wealth for *their* children.
¹⁵ And me? When I look at justice I see your face;
    and when I awake, I'll be content just to see your likeness.

18

For the conductor
By David, God's faithful one, who sang Adonai this song
the day God saved him from the hand of all his enemies—
from the hand of Saul. This is what he sang:

¹ I love you, Adonai,
    my strength.
² Adonai—
    my mountain crag,
    my fortress,
    my rescuer,
    my God,
    my rock behind whom I take refuge,
    my shield,
    my horn of deliverance,
    my stronghold!
³ The One whom I praise,
    and to whom I call,
is Adonai—
    and from the enemy I am saved!

⁴ The waves of Death enclosed me,
    the torrents of Destruction devoured me;
⁵ the snares of Sheol entangled me,
    the traps of Death drew me down.

6 In my distress I called you, Adonai;
    to you, my God, I cried for help.

    From your Temple you heard my voice,
        and my cry to you reached your ears.
7 Then the netherworld reeled and rocked;
        the mountains trembled to their foundations
        in the presence of your anger.
8 Smoke billowed from your nostrils
        and a consuming fire spewed forth from your mouth;
        glowing coals erupted into flames.
9 You tore through the heavens and came down;
        thick darkness was under your feet.
10 You rode upon the backs of cherubim,
        and soared on the wings of the wind.
11 You made the night your cloak;
        you covered yourself in a canopy of storm clouds.
12 From the brightness before you
        your clouds surged forth
        with hailstones and lightning bolts.
13 You thundered in the heavens,
        and your voice, Most High, resounded
        with hailstones and bolts of lightning.
14 You shot your arrows and scattered my enemies;
        you scattered your lightning bolts and routed them.
15 Then the channels of the sea were exposed,
        and the foundations of the world were laid bare
    at your rebuke, Adonai,
        at a snort from your nostrils.
16 You reached from on high and took hold of me,
        and pulled me out of deep water.
17 You rescued me from my strong enemy,
        and from my foes who were too powerful for me.
18 They fell upon me in the day of my calamity,
        but you, Adonai, were my support.
19 You brought me out of the vast netherworld;
        you rescued me, because you delighted in me.

20 Adonai, you set everything right again because I was just;
        you rewarded me because my hands were clean.
21 For I kept your ways, Adonai:
        I didn't do evil—I didn't leave you, my God.

22 For all your laws were in front of me,
    and I didn't turn away from a single decree.
23 I was blameless before you,
    and I kept myself from evil—
24 you rewarded me because I was just,
    because I kept my hands clean.

25 To those who love,
    you show yourself loving;
to those who are blameless,
    you show yourself blameless;
26 to those who are single-hearted,
    you show yourself single-hearted;
to those who are crooked,
    you show yourself...shrewd!
27 You save humble people,
    but force the arrogant to lower their eyes.
28 You are my ever-burning lamp, Adonai!
    My God, you lighten my darkness!
29 Yes, with you I can crush a brigade,
    and with my God I can scale ramparts.

30 O God, your way is perfect;
    your promise, Adonai, proves true:
    you are a shield for all who take refuge in you.
31 For who is God, but you?
    And who is a rock except our God?—
32 the God who arms me with strength
    and makes my path perfectly safe,
33 who gives me the sure footing of a mountain goat,
    and sets me on heights of my own,
34 who trains my hands for battle
    so that my arms can bend a bow of bronze.
35 You have given me your shield of victory
    and your strong hand supported me;
    you stoop to make me great.
36 You make my road wide and smooth,
    so that I never twist an ankle.

37 I pursued my enemies and overtook them,
    and did not relent until they were destroyed.
38 I crushed them, so they couldn't get up;
    they fell beneath my feet.

39 For you armed me with strength for the battle;
    you made my assailants sink beneath me.
40 You made my enemies turn back and run,
    and I destroyed my opponents.
41 They cried for help, but there was none to save them;
    they cried to God, but God didn't answer them.
42 I beat them as fine as dust in the square;
    I stomped on them like mud in the streets.
43 You delivered me from the attacks of an unbelieving people;
    you made me a leader of the nations.
    A people whom I had not known
    are now subject to me.
44 As soon as they hear of me, they obey me—
    nations come cringing!
45 The nations come cowering,
    and come trembling from their strongholds.

46 Our God lives! Blessed be my rock!
    And let the God of my salvation be exalted—
47 the God who gave me vengeance
    and subdued my attackers under me,
48   who delivered me from defamers!
49 For this I will extol you among the nations, Adonai,
    and sing praises to your Name.
50 You give great victories to your leader,
    and show unfailing love to your Anointed,
    to David and his descendants forever.

19

For the conductor
A psalm of David

1 The heavens herald your glory, O God,
  and the skies display your handiwork.
2 Day after day they tell their story,
  and night after night they reveal
  the depth of their understanding.
3 Without speech, without words,
  without even an audible voice,
4 their cry echoes through all the world,
  and their message reaches the ends of the earth.
  For in the heavens
  the sun has pitched a tent.
5 It comes forth with the grandeur of a wedding procession,
  with the eagerness of an athlete ready to race.
6 It rises at one end of the sky
  and travels to the other end,
  and nothing escapes its warmth.

7 Your law, Adonai, is perfect;
  it refreshes the soul.
  Your rule is to be trusted;
  it gives wisdom to the naive.
8 Your purposes, O God, are right;
  they gladden the heart.
  Your command is clear;
  it gives light to the eyes.
9 Holding you in awe, Adonai, is purifying;
  it endures.
  Your decrees are steadfast,
  and all of them just.
10 They are more precious than gold,
  than the purest of gold,
  and sweeter than honey,
  than honey fresh from the comb.
11 In them your faithful people find instruction;
  there is great reward in keeping them.

¹² But who can detect one's own failings?
Forgive the misdeeds I don't even know about!
¹³ Keep your faithful one from presumption as well,
so that my faults never control me.
Then I will be blameless
and innocent of a grave error.

¹⁴ May the words of my mouth
and the thoughts of my heart
be pleasing in your sight, Adonai,
my rock and my redeemer!

20

¹ May Our God answer you in the day of distress!
May the Name of the God
of Leah, Rachel and Jacob protect you!
² May God send you help from the sanctuary
and sustain you from Zion!
³ May God remember all your sacrifices,
and accept your burnt offerings!
—— *Selah* ——
⁴ May God give you your heart's desires
and fulfill all your dreams!
⁵ We will shout for joy over your triumph
and in the Name of our God wave our banners—
may Our God grant all your petitions!

⁶ Now I know that Our God saves the anointed,
answering from holy heaven with saving power.
⁷ Some trust in political power, some in military might,
but we trust in the Name of Adonai, our God!
⁸ With only human resources, they fall;
but we have risen, and we stand firm.

⁹ Save us, Adonai, our Ruler!
Answer when we call.

For the conductor
A psalm of David

1 This ruler, Adonai, rejoices in your strength!
       How great is my joy in your victory!
2 You've given me my heart's desire
       and did not deny me the wish of my lips.
                    —— *Selah* ——
3 You greeted me with lavish blessings,
       and placed on my head a crown of pure gold.
4 I asked you for life;
       you gave me length of days forever and ever.
5 Great is my glory in your victory;
       you bestowed majesty and splendor upon me.
6 You gave me a boon forever:
       you gladdened me with the joy of your presence.
7 For this ruler trusts in you, Adonai;
       because of your love, I stand unshaken.

8 May your hand reach all my enemies,
       your right hand reach my foes!
9 They'll look like a fiery furnace when you appear—
       you, O God, will consume them in anger,
       and fire will devour them.
10 You'll wipe their progeny from the earth,
       their posterity from among the peoples.
11 Though they concoct heinous plots against you,
       the schemes they devise cannot succeed—
12 for you will put them to flight
       and all they will see
       are your arrows flying at them.

13 Be exalted, Adonai, in your strength!
       We will sing the praise of your might!

22

To the conductor: to the tune of "Doe of the Morning"
A psalm of David

1 My God, my God,
   why have you forsaken me?
Why are you so far away,
   so far from saving me,
   so far from the words of my groaning?
2 I cry all day, my God, but you never answer;
   I call all night long, and sleep deserts me.

3 But you, Holy One—
   you sit enthroned on the praises of Israel.
4 Our ancestors put their trust in you,
   they trusted and you rescued them;
5 they cried to you and were saved,
   they trusted you and were never disappointed.

6 Yet here I am, more worm than human,
   the scorn of humanity, an object of ridicule:
7 all who see me mock me,
   they shake their heads and sneer,
8 "You trust in God? Ha! Let God save you now!
   If God is your friend, let God rescue you!"
9 Yet you drew me out of the womb,
   you nestled me in my mother's bosom;
10 you cradled me in your lap from my birth,
   from my mother's womb you have been my God.
11 Don't stand aside now that trouble is near—
   I have no one to help me!

12 My enemies are like a herd of bulls surrounding me,
   like the strong bulls of Bashan closing in on me;
13 with jaws open wide to swallow me,
   they're like lions tearing their prey, and roaring.
14 I am like water draining away,
   my bones are all disjointed,
   my heart is like wax melting inside me.
15 My strength is dried up like a piece of clay pottery
   and my tongue is stuck to the roof of my mouth:
   you lay me down in dusty death.

16 A pack of dogs surrounds me,
   a gang of brigands close me in;
   they pierce my hands and feet.
17 I can count every one of my bones,
   and there they stare at me, gloating.
18 They divide my garments among them
   and cast lots for my clothes.

19 But you, Adonai, don't be far off!
   My strength, hurry to help me!
20 Rescue my life from the sword,
   my dear life from the power of these dogs!
21 Save me from the lion's mouth,
   my poor soul from the wild bull's horns!

22 Then I will proclaim your Name to my sisters and brothers,
   and praise you in the full assembly:
23 "You who worship Our God, give praise!
   Daughters of Leah, daughters of Rachel, glorify Our God!
   Sons of Jacob, fall down and worship!
24 For God has not despised—not disdained—
   the suffering of those in pain!
   God didn't hide
   but answered them when they cried for help!"
25 You are the theme of my praise in the Great Assembly,
   and I will fulfill my vows in the presence of your worshipers.
26 Those who are poor will eat and be satisfied,
   those who seek you will give you praise—
   long life to their hearts!
27 The whole earth, from one end to the other,
   will remember and come back to you;
   all the families of the nations
   will bow down to you.
28 For yours is the kindom,
   you Ruler of nations!
29 Those who had feasted and devoured the poor—
   now they'll bow down;
   the most affluent in the land
   will kneel before you.
   They all go down to the dust
   and none can keep themselves alive.

30 But my children will be faithful to you,
        and they will be told about Our God for generations to come.
31 They will come and proclaim your justice
        to a people yet unborn:
        "All this Our God has done!"

23

A psalm of David

1 Adonai, you are my shepherd—
        I want nothing more.
2 You let me lie down in green meadows,
        you lead me beside restful waters:
3   you refresh my soul.
    You guide me to lush pastures
        for the sake of your Name.
4 Even if I'm surrounded by shadows of Death,
        I fear no danger,
        for you are with me.
    Your rod and your staff—
        they give me courage.
5 You spread a table for me
        in the presence of my enemies,
    and you anoint my head with oil—
        my cup overflows!
6 Only goodness and love will follow me
        all the days of my life,
    and I will dwell in your house, Adonai,
        for days without end.

1 The earth and everything on it—
   the world and all who live in it—
   belong to Our God.
2 Our God built it on the deep waters,
   laying its foundations in the ocean depths.

3 Who has the right to ascend Our God's mountain?
   Who is allowed to enter Our God's holy place?
4 Those whose hands are clean and whose hearts are pure,
   who do not worship idols, or make false promises.
5 Our God will bless them;
   God their savior will declare them innocent.
6 Such are the people who seek Our God,
   who seek your face, God of our ancestors.
   —— *Selah* ——

7 Fling wide the gates,
   open the ancient doors,
   and the Glorious Liberator will come in!
8 Who is this "Glorious Liberator"?
   Adonai, strong and mighty,
   Our God, victorious in battle!
9 Fling wide the gates,
   open the ancient doors,
   and the Glorious Liberator will come in!
10 Who is this "Glorious Liberator"?
   Adonai Sabaoth is our Glorious Liberator!
   —— *Selah* ——

1   To you, Adonai,
       I lift up my soul.
2   My God, I trust in you;
       don't let me be ashamed,
       don't let my enemies triumph over me.
3   No—none who hope in you will be ashamed,
       but shame will come to the wantonly treacherous.

4   Show me your ways, Adonai!
       Teach me your paths!
5   Lead me in your truth and teach me,
       for you are the God of my salvation.
       I wait all the day long for you.
6   Remember your mercies, Adonai, your love—
       your ancient and unwavering love!
7   Pardon the sins of my youth
       and my rebellious ways;
    remember me because of your love,
       because of your goodness, Adonai!

8   And how good and upright you are, Adonai!
       You instruct sinners in the path,
9   you guide the humble in what is right,
       and teach them your way.
10   All of your paths, Adonai,
       are full of love and faithfulness
       for those who keep your Covenant and Testimonies.

11   For the sake of your Name, Adonai,
       pardon my guilt, for it is great.
12   Who are those who revere you?
       They are the ones you teach
       which way you want them to go.
13   Their lives will be spent in prosperity,
       and their children will possess the land.
14   Our God becomes friends with those who show reverence,
       and reveals the Covenant to them.

15 My eyes are always on you, Adonai,
    for you will pluck my feet out of the snare.
16 Turn to me, be gracious to me,
    for I am lonely and anguished.
17 How heavy are the troubles of my heart!
    Free me from my distress!
18 Look at my affliction and my trouble,
    and mend all my brokenness.
19 See how my enemies keep multiplying,
    how they hate me so violently!
20 O guard of my life, rescue me!
    Don't let me be put to shame,
    for I take refuge in you.
21 May integrity and uprightness protect me,
    for you are my only hope.

22 Ransom Israel, O God,
    from all trouble!

By David

1 Do me justice, Adonai!
    For I have walked in integrity
    and I have trusted in you without wavering.
2 Search me, Adonai, and test me;
    examine my heart and my mind.
3 For your love is before my eyes,
    and I walk in your truth.
4 I don't sit with deceitful people,
    nor do I consort with hypocrites.
5 I avoid places where troublemakers gather,
    and have nothing to do with violent people.
6 I wash my hands in innocence
    and minister at your altar, Adonai,
7 giving voice to my praise
    and recounting all your wondrous deeds.
8 Adonai, I love the house in which you dwell,
    the dwelling place of your glory.
9 Don't sweep me away with sinners,
    or take my life along with the bloodthirsty!
10 They hatch terrible schemes with their left hand,
    and take bribes with their right.
11 But I walk in integrity;
    ransom me, and have pity on me.
12 My foot stands on level ground;
    in the assemblies I will bless Adonai.

27

By David

1 Adonai, you are my light, my salvation—
   whom will I fear?
You are the fortress of my life—
   of whom will I be afraid?
2 When my enemies attack me,
   spreading vicious lies about me wherever they go,
they, my adversaries and foes,
   will stumble and fall.
3 Though an army mounts a siege against me,
   my heart will not fear;
though war break out against me,
   I'll still be confident.

4 One thing I ask of you, Adonai,
   one thing I seek:
that I may dwell in your house
   all the days of my life,
to gaze on your beauty
   and to meditate in your Temple.
5 You will keep me safe in your shelter
   when trouble arises,
you will hide me under the cover of your Tabernacle—
   you'll set me on a rock, high and out of reach.
6 Then I'll be able to hold my head up,
   even with my enemies surrounding me.
I will offer in your Tabernacle
   sacrifices of great joy—
   I'll sing and make music to you, Adonai!

7 Hear me when I call, Adonai!
   Have mercy on me and answer me!
8 You say to my heart, "Seek my face,"
   and so it is your face I seek!
9 Don't hide your face from me,
   don't turn your faithful one away in anger.
Don't reject me, don't desert me,
   O God of my salvation,
   for you are my only help.

10 Even if my own parents reject me,
    you, Adonai, will accept me.
11 Teach me your way, Adonai,
    and lead me on a straight path because of my enemies.
12 Don't surrender me to the will of my enemies;
    for defamers rise up against me breathing violence.

13 Even so I have confidence
    that I'll see the goodness of Our God
    in the land of the living!
14 Wait for God—stand tall
    and let your heart take courage!
    Yes, wait for Our God!

28

By David

1 To you, Adonai, I call—
    my rock, don't turn a deaf ear to me!
If you don't heed my cry,
    I'll become like those who go to the Pit.
2 Hear the voice of my pleading
    as I call to you for help,
as I lift up my hands in prayer
    toward your Most Holy Place!
3 Don't drag me away with the violent,
    with the evildoers,
who speak words of peace to their neighbors
    but have evil in their hearts.
4 Repay them as their actions deserve,
    for the malice of their deeds
and for the work of their hands—
    give them their deserts!
5 For they ignore your deeds, Adonai
    and the work of your hands.

6 I will bless you, Adonai, for you have heard
    my cries for mercy.

7 You are my strength and my shield;
 in you my heart trusts.
You revived me—my heart rejoices,
 and I praise you with my song.
8 You are the strength of your people,
 the stronghold where your anointed find salvation.
9 Save your people, and bless Israel your inheritance!
 Be their shepherd and carry them forever!

29

A psalm of David

1 Give glory to Our God, you heavenly court,
 give Our God glory and strength!
2 Give forth the glory that God's Name deserves,
 and worship Our God in the splendor of holiness!

3 The voice of Our God resounds over the waters;
 the God of glory thunders over the raging seas.
4 God's voice is powerful,
 God's voice is full of majesty.
5 The voice of Our God snaps the cedars,
 shatters the cedars of Lebanon.
6 It makes Lebanon skip like a calf,
 and Sirion like a young wild ox.
7 The voice of Our God strikes with bolts of lightning;
8 the voice of Our God shakes the wilderness,
 the wilderness of Kadesh.
9 The voice of God twists the oaks,
 and strips the forests bare;
 and in God's Temple all cry, "Glory!"
10 Our God sits in judgment over the flood;
 Adonai is its Ruler forever.
11 Give strength to your people, Adonai!
 Bless your people with peace!

30

A psalm
A song for the dedication of the Temple
By David

1 I praise you, O God, because you raised me up
    and kept my enemies from gloating over me.
2 I cried to you for help, Adonai my God,
    and you healed me.
3 You brought me back from the realm of the dead, Adonai;
    you spared me from going down into the Pit.

4 Sing to Adonai, you who love God!
    Praise God's holy Name!
5 Our God's anger is fleeting,
    but God's favor endures forever.
  There may be tears during the night,
    but joy comes in the morning.

6 When I presumed I was secure, I boasted,
    "I will never be defeated!"
7 When I stood in your favor, Adonai,
    I stood as firm as a mountain.
  But then you hid yourself from me,
    and I was filled with terror.
8 So I called to you, Adonai,
    I pleaded for your help:
9 "What good will come from my destruction,
    from my going to the grave?
  Does dust praise you, Adonai?
    Can the dead proclaim your unfailing goodness?
10 Hear me, Adonai, and be merciful!
    Help me, Adonai!"

11 Then you changed my despair into a dance—
    you stripped me of my death shroud
    and clothed me with joy.
12 That's why my heart sings to you,
    that's why I can't keep silent—
  Adonai, you are my God,
    and I will thank you forever!

1   In you, Adonai, I took refuge;
        never let me be disgraced!
        In your justice, deliver me!
2   Turn your ear to me!
        Hurry! Rescue me!
    Be the rock I hide behind,
        be the walled fortress that saves me!
3   Because you are my rock, my fortress,
        and for the sake of your Name,
        lead me, guide me!
4   Pull me out of the trap they set for me,
        for you are my refuge!

5   Into your hands I commit my spirit;
        deliver me, Adonai, God of truth!
6   I hate those who cling to useless idols;
        but I trust in you.
7   I'll be happy,
        I'll rejoice in your love—
    for you saw my despair,
        you knew the dark night of my soul.
8   You didn't hand me over to the enemy,
        but gave my feet boundless freedom.

9   Now take pity on me, Adonai,
        for I'm in trouble again.
    I cried so much that I'm exhausted—
        and not only my eyes, but my mind and body as well.
10 My life is consumed by sorrow,
        my years are worn out with my sighs;
    my strength fails me because of my despair,
        my bones are getting weaker.
11 Because of all my oppressors
        I'm held in utter contempt, even by my neighbors;
    my friends are afraid of me,
        and people who see me on the street hurry past me.
12 I am forgotten, as good as dead in their hearts,
        like something that has outlived its usefulness.

13 I hear their endless slanders,
    and threats from every quarter
as they conspire against me,
    plotting to take my life.

14 But I put my trust in you, Adonai;
    I say, "You are my God!"
15 My times are in your hand,
    save me from the hands of my enemies and persecutors.
16 Smile on your faithful one,
    save me in your love!
17 Don't let me be disgraced, Adonai,
    for I cried to you;
 let disgrace fall instead on the corrupt—
    in their silence, let them go to Sheol,
18 their lying lips sealed shut
    because of their sneering contempt for those who do right,
    because of their overwhelming pride and arrogance.

19 How great is the goodness
    reserved for those who revere you!
You bestow it—in front of everyone—
    on those who take refuge in you.
20 Safe in your presence,
    you hide them from the world's insidious schemes;
inside your tent, you shelter them,
    far from the war of tongues!
21 Blessed are you, Adonai,
    for you showed your wonderful love to me
    in a city under siege!
22 In my alarm I exclaimed,
    "I've been snatched from your sight!"
Yet you heard the sound of my cries
    when I called to you for help.

23 Revel in your love for God,
    you whom God has touched!
For Our God protects the faithful
    but will repay the arrogant in full.
24 Be strong, let your heart be bold,
    you who hope in Our God.

32

By David
A teaching poem

1 Happiness comes from having your rebellion taken away,
    from having your failure completely covered.
2 Happiness comes from Our God not counting your mistakes,
    from having nothing to hide.
3 As long as I kept my stubborn silence,
    my bones grew weak because of my constant complaints.
4 Day and night your hand was heavy upon me;
    my strength was sapped by a summer's heat.
    —— *Selah* ——
5 Finally I admitted my sin to you,
    and stopped hiding my guilt.
I said, "I confess my rebellion, Adonai,"
    and you took away the guilt of my sin.
    —— *Selah* ——
6 That's why people of faith everywhere
    should pray to you—they'll find you.
Even when the flood begins rising,
    it will never touch them.
7 You are my hiding place;
    you'll protect me from trouble
    and surround me with songs of freedom.
    —— *Selah* ——

8 "I'll teach you
    and show you the way you should walk;
I will counsel you,
    and keep watch over you.
9 Be wise!
    Don't be like horses and mules,
who need to be harnessed with bit and bridle
    before they'll come to you."

10 Wrongdoers are prone to many sorrows,
    but those who trust in Our God
    are surrounded with unfailing love.
11 Be glad in Our God and rejoice, you who love justice!
    Exult, you upright of heart!

1 Sing out your joy to Our God, you who love justice—
   praise is fitting for loyal hearts.
2 Praise Our God with the harp,
   and play music with a ten-stringed lyre!
3 Sing God a new song,
   play with all your skill, and with shouts of joy!
4 For the word of Our God is true
   and everything God does can be trusted.
5 Our God loves justice and right
   and fills the earth with love.

6 By your word, Adonai, the heavens were made,
   by the breath of your mouth all the stars.
7 You gather the seas together and control them,
   putting the Deep into its vault.
8 Let all the earth revere Our God,
   let all who live in the world tremble before you!
9 You spoke, and everything came to be;
   commanded, and it all sprang into being.
10 You frustrate the designs of the nations,
   defeat the plans of the peoples.
11 But your own plan will stand firm forever,
   the designs of your heart from age to age.
12 Happy is the nation whose God is Adonai!
   Happy the people you choose as your own inheritance!
13 From the heavens you look forth, Adonai,
   and see all of humankind.
14 From your dwelling place you watch over
   all the peoples of the earth.
15 You shape the hearts of them all
   and consider all their deeds.

16 A ruler isn't saved by the size of an army;
   a warrior doesn't escape because of strength.
17 Trust in the horse for your deliverance
   and you'll be disappointed—
despite its might,
   it cannot save.
18 The eyes of Our God look on those who stand in reverence,
   on those who hope in God's love

19 to rescue them from death,
   or to keep them alive during famine.
20 And so we wait for Our God,
   our help and our shield.
21 For in you our hearts find joy;
   we trust in your holy Name.
22 May your love be upon us, Adonai,
   as we place all our hope in you.

34*

By David
Written when he pretended to be insane in front of Abimelech,
who drove him away and he escaped

1 I will bless Our God always,
   praise will continually be on my lips!
2 My soul will boast about Our God—
   let the oppressed hear it and be glad!
3 Glorify Our God with me,
   and let us exalt God's Name together!
4 I sought Our God, who answered me
   and freed me from all my fears.
5 Those who look to Our God are radiant,
   and their faces are never covered with shame.
6 The poor called out; Our God heard
   and saved them from all their troubles.
7 The angel of Our God encamps around those
   who revere God, and rescues them.
8 Taste and see how good Our God is!
   Happiness comes to those who take refuge in Our God.
9 Holy people of God, revere Adonai—
   for those who stand in awe of God lack nothing.
10 The young lion may grow weak and hungry,
   but those who seek Our God will lack no good thing.

---

* This psalm is an acrostic poem: the first letter of each verse begins with a subsequent letter of the Hebrew alphabet.

11 Come, children, listen to me!
    I will teach you reverence for Our God.
12 Which of you loves life,
    and wants to enjoy a long life of prosperity?
13 Then keep your tongue from gossip
    and your lips from telling lies;
14 turn away from bad and practice good;
    seek peace and pursue it.

15 The eyes of Our God are on those who do justice,
    and God's ears are open to their cry.
16 The face of Our God is turned against evildoers
    to cut off their memory from the earth.
17 But the just cry out, and Our God hears,
    and saves them from all their troubles.
18 Our God is close to the brokenhearted ·
    and rescues those whose spirits are crushed.
19 Many are the afflictions of the just;
    but Our God delivers them from all their troubles.
20 Our God protects their very bones,
    and not one of them will be broken.
21 Calamity will strike down these vicious curs,
    and the haters of justice will be condemned.
22 Our God ransoms the lives of the faithful,
    and none who take refuge in God will see punishment.

1   Accuse my accusers, Adonai,
        attack my attackers!
2   Grip your shield and sword,
        arise and help me!
3   Brandish your spear and javelin
        in the faces of my pursuers!
    Say to me,
        "I am your victory!"

4   Shame and infamy on those
        who are out to kill me!
    Turn them back,
        and confuse those who plot my downfall!
5   Let them be like chaff in the wind,
        with the angel of Our God driving them!
6   Let them walk a dark and slippery road
        with the angel of Our God hounding their heels!
7   Without provocation, they spread their net for me;
        unprovoked, they dug a pit for me.
8   But let ruin overtake them unawares—
        let the net they spread for me catch them instead,
        let them fall into their own pit.

9   Then I'll rejoice in Our God,
        exult that God has saved me.
10 All my bones will exclaim,
        "Adonai, who can compare to you?
    You rescue the oppressed from their oppressors,
        the vulnerable from their exploiters!"

11 Perjurers take the stand against me;
        people I don't even know accuse me falsely.
12 They repay my kindness with violence,
        and I am left desolate.
13 Yet when they were sick, I wore sackcloth;
        I even humbled my soul with fasting
        when my prayers for them went unanswered.
14 I went around weeping for them like a grieving parent,
        I mourned as though for a friend or relative.

15 But when I stumbled, they were full of glee,
    and flocked to jeer at me;
  strangers I never even knew flocked to the stand,
    to deride and slander me without ceasing;
16 my treacherous foes circled around me,
    mocking me and grinding their teeth at me.

17 How much longer, Adonai, will you look on?
    Rescue me from their onslaughts,
    my dear life from these lions!
18 I will give thanks in the Great Assembly,
    praise you where the people throng.
19 Don't let these liars gloat over me,
    don't let those who hate me for no reason
    exchange sly glances!
20 They do not speak of peace,
    but attack the most vulnerable of the land.
21 They hatch vicious plans to slander me,
    and spread lies about me through the land—
  "Aha! Aha!" they say.
    "With our own eyes we witnessed your crime!"

22 But you're the one, Adonai, who witnessed everything.
    Don't remain silent, don't be far from me!
23 Wake up! Arise to my defense!
    Adonai, my God, side with me!
24 Vindicate me in your justice, Adonai my God,
    and don't let them gloat over me.
25 Don't let them think,
    "We've got you just where we wanted!"
  Don't let them say,
    "We've swallowed you whole!"
26 Let all who gloat over my misfortune
    be put to shame and confusion;
  let all who profit at my expense
    be clothed with shame and infamy!

27 But let those who delight in my vindication
    shout for joy and be glad;
  let those who delight in the well-being of your faithful one
    continually say, "Our God be praised!"
28 Then my tongue will tell of your justice,
    and sing your praises all day long.

36

For the conductor
By David, loyal subject of Our God

1 Deep in the heart of the violent,
    perversity is the only oracle they hear.
  They never view God
    with awe or reverence.
2 They flatter themselves in their own eyes so much
    that they can't see—can't hate—their own guilt.
3 In their mouths are mischief and deceit;
    all wisdom, all goodness is gone.
4 They hatch devious plots
    as they lie on their beds.
  They set their feet on ways that aren't good;
    they cling to what is evil.

5 Your love, Adonai, reaches to the heavens,
    your faithfulness to the skies.
6 Your justice is like the mountains in their splendor,
    Your judgments like the great deep.
  Whether human or animal, Adonai,
    you keep us all in your care.
7 How precious is your love!
  Whether creatures of heaven or children of earth,
    we all find refuge in the shadow of your wings.
8 We feast on the bounty of your estate,
    and drink from the stream of your delights.
9 In you is the wellspring of Life,
    and in your light we become enlightened.
10 Prolong your love for those who know you,
    and your justice for upright hearts.

11 Don't let the foot of the proud crush me
    nor the hand of the evildoer drive me away.
12 See how the violent have fallen—
    Flung down, unable to rise again!

37 *

By David

1   Don't be vexed by evildoers,
     and don't be envious of the corrupt!
2   They'll soon fade like the grass,
     and wither away like unwatered plants.

3   Trust in Our God, and do good,
     and you'll dwell in the land and enjoy security.
4   Delight in Adonai,
     and you'll be given the desires of your heart.

5   Commit your way to Adonai, and trust in Our God;
     God *will* take action,
6   making your vindication as sure as the dawn
     and your integrity as bright as noonday.

7   Be still before Our God and wait patiently;
     don't fret about those who amass great fortunes
     and carry out their schemes unchallenged.

8   Let go of your anger,
     and leave resentment behind.
  And stop worrying!
     It produces nothing but evil,
9   and evildoers will be cut off.
  But those who put their hope in Our God—
     they will inherit the land.

10   A little while longer,
     and the violent will be no more;
  no matter how hard you look for them,
     they will not be found.
11   But the gentle will inherit the land,
     and will enjoy abundant peace.

12   Unscrupulous people plot against the just,
     and gnash their teeth at them;

---

* This psalm is an acrostic poem: the first letter of each stanza begins with a subsequent letter of the Hebrew alphabet.

13 but the Sovereign One laughs at them,
   knowing that their day is coming.

14 They draw their sword and bend their bow
   to slaughter the poor and needy,
   to murder those who walk uprightly;
15 but they will be pierced through the heart with their own sword,
   and their bows will be broken.

16 Better the little that honest people have saved
   than the ill-gotten gains amassed by the corrupt.
17 The power of the corrupt will be broken;
   but Our God champions the just.

18 Our God safeguards the possessions of the honest,
   and their inheritance will last forever;
19 they will not wither in the days of drought,
   and when famine comes, they will have abundance.

20 But the corrupt will shrivel up;
   the enemies of Our God are like blazing fields—they vanish,
   they vanish more quickly than smoke.

21 The corrupt borrow and never pay back,
   but the righteous are generous and giving;
22 for those blessed by God will inherit the land,
   but the accursed will be slashed down.

23 Our steps are steadied by Adonai,
   who secures our path.
24 Though we stumble, we won't fall,
   for God is holding our hand.

25 I was once young, and now I am old;
   but I have never seen the just forsaken
   nor their children begging bread.
26 All day long they're generous and lend willingly,
   and their children become a blessing.

27 Turn from evil and do good,
   and you'll always live securely.
28 For Our God loves justice
   and will never forsake the faithful,
   but the progeny of the corrupt will be cut down.

²⁹ The just will inherit the land,
   and dwell in it forever.

³⁰ The mouth of the just utters wisdom,
   and their tongue speaks justice.
³¹ The Law of God is in their heart;
   their feet don't slip.

³² Violent criminals lie in ambush for the just,
   and seek to massacre them.
³³ But Our God will not surrender them
      to the power of evil,
   or let them be condemned
      when they're brought to trial.

³⁴ Wait for Adonai, and keep Our God's way,
      and God will raise you up
   so that you can possess the land,
      where you will witness the destruction of the corrupt.

³⁵ I have witnessed the corrupt become powerful,
   and flourish like trees born for this soil.
³⁶ Then suddenly they vanished and were gone—
   I looked for them, but they couldn't be found.

³⁷ But take note of the blameless—behold the upright,
   for there is a future for peacemakers.
³⁸ But those who insist on rebellion will be utterly destroyed;
   the future of the corrupt will be cut short.

³⁹ The safety of the just is from Our God,
   their refuge when trouble comes.
⁴⁰ Adonai helps them and rescues them—
   rescues them from the violent and saves them,
   because they take refuge in Our God.

A psalm of David
A supplication

1 Adonai, don't rebuke me in your anger
      or chastise me in your wrath!
2 For your arrows hit their mark,
      and I've felt the blows from your hand.
3 There is no health in my body
      because of your indignation;
   there is no wholeness to my bones
      because of my sin.
4 For my guilt has overwhelmed me;
      it's a heavy burden, too onerous for me to carry.
5 My wounds stink and fester;
      and all because I was such a fool.
6 I am completely broken;
      bent low, I walk around in anguish all day.
7 For my loins are filled with inflammation,
      and there is no health to my body.
8 I am utterly exhausted and crushed;
      I scream because my heart and mind are filled with discord.
9 Adonai, you know everything I long for,
      and my groans aren't hidden from you.
10 My heart is fever-racked, my strength fails me;
      even my eyes look dull and dead.
11 My friends and companions avoid me like the plague,
      and my neighbors stay far away.
12 Those who seek my life lay their snares,
      the ones who want to hurt me threaten ruin
      and plot their treachery all day long.
13 But I act like I'm deaf and can't hear,
      like I'm mute and can't speak:
14 I don't listen to what they're saying,
      and there are no retorts in my mouth.
15 It's because I wait for you, Adonai,
      and you'll answer me, my God, my Sovereign.
16 I said, "Don't let them gloat over me,
      don't let them get the advantage when my foot slips!"

17 But now I'm ready to fall,
   and my pain never leaves me.
18 I confess my transgression,
   I am sorry that I rebelled against you.
19 I have many mortal enemies,
   and those who hate me without reason are numerous.
20 Those who repay good with evil
   slander me for pursuing good.
21 Don't desert me too!
   My God, don't be far away from me!
22 Hurry and help me,
   my Sovereign, my Liberator!

For the conductor
Dedicated to Jeduthun
A psalm of David

1 I said, "I'll watch my words
  so that I don't stumble over my tongue.
I'll muzzle my mouth
  whenever corrupt people are nearby."
2 So I stood silent and still
  not even saying anything good—
  and my anguish began to grow.
3 My heart grew hot inside me,
  my thoughts burned like a fire—
  until I finally spoke:

4 Show me my end, Adonai!
  How many more days do I have?
  How fleeting is my life?
5 My life is as short as a hand's breadth,
  its span is nothing in your sight.
Each person is a mere mist;
  everyone's life but a fading mirage.
    —— *Selah* ——
6 People roam through the streets like ghosts,
  in restless pursuit of vainglory;
they build storehouses of great wealth,
  without thought of who will get
  their fortune after they vanish.

7 But now, my God, what is there to wait for?
  You are everything I hope for.
8 Set me free from all my sins;
  don't make me the taunt of fools!
9 I was silent, not opening my mouth,
  because this was all your doing.
10 Put away the whips you've used on me;
  I'm crushed by the blows of your hand.
11 You discipline people
  and correct them because of their error—

like the moth, you devour everything they treasure;
    each person is a mere mist.
12 Hear my prayer, Adonai, and my cry for help!
    Listen to my weeping, and don't ignore me.
    I'm an alien with you, a stranger, as were all my ancestors.
13 Look away from me and let me rejoice once again,
    or I'll leave this life and be no more!

40

For the conductor
A psalm of David

1 Unyielding, I called to you, Adonai,
    now at last you have stooped to me
    and answered my cry for help.
2 You have pulled me out of the Pit of Destruction,
    out of its mud and quicksand;
you set my feet on a rock
    and made my steps firm.
3 You put a new song in my mouth,
    a song of praise to you.
Many will look on in wonder
    and so will put their trust in you.
4 Happiness comes to those
    who put their trust in Our God,
instead of in human egos
    or people blind to the truth!

5 How many wonders you've worked for us,
    Adonai, my God!
 How many plans you've made for us;
    you have no equal!
I want to recount them again and again,
    but their number is too great.
6 You don't desire sacrifice or oblation,
    instead you made my ears receptive to you;
you asked no burnt offering
    or sacrifice for sins from me.

7 And so I declared,
   "Here I am! I have come!
8 In the scroll of the book
   it is written about me."
   I desire to do your will, my God,
   and your law is written in my heart.
9 I'll proclaim your justice
   in the Great Assembly,
   and I won't keep my mouth shut,
   as you well know.
10 I have never kept your generosity to myself,
   but announce your faithfulness and saving action;
   I have made no secret of your love and faithfulness
   in the Great Assembly.

11 For your part, Adonai, don't withhold your love from me!
   Let your kindness and faithfulness constantly protect me!
12 Misfortunes surround me, far more than I can count;
   my sins entrap me and I am unable to escape.
   They outnumber the hairs on my head,
   and my courage is drained.
13 Hurry! Come to my rescue, Adonai!
   Be swift to help me!

14 Shame and confusion on all
   who are out to destroy me!
   Turn them back and heap disgrace
   on those who enjoy my misfortune!
15 May they be horrified at their shame,
   those who say to me, "Aha! Aha!"
16 May there be joy and gladness
   for all who seek you!
   May all who love your saving power
   have constant cause to say, "God is great!"

17 Now I am poor and needy.
   May Adonai think of me!
   You are my helper and deliverer—
   come swiftly!

41

For the conductor
A psalm of David

1 Happiness comes to those who tell the truth;
   Our God will defend them when they are in trouble.
2 Our God will protect and preserve them,
   giving them long life and happiness in the land,
   and will not abandon them to the desires of their enemies.
3 Our God will nourish them on their sickbed,
   and restore them to health.
4 I said, "Have mercy on me, Adonai, and heal me,
   for I have rebelled against you!"

5 My enemies spew curses at me,
   like, "Why don't you just die
   and disappear along with your name!"
6 Those who visit me are duplicitous;
   they come only to gather bad news about me,
   and when they leave, they gossip everywhere.
7 My enemies whisper to each other behind my back;
   they fabricate horrible lies about me.
8 They say, "You have a vile disease
   and you'll never leave your bed again!"
9 Even my best friend, the one I trusted most,
   the one who broke bread at my table,
   spins slanderous tales about me.

10 Be merciful to me, Adonai!
   Raise me up so that I can pay them back!
11 I will know you're pleased with me
   if my enemy doesn't triumph over me.
12 You uphold me through my integrity,
   and set me in your presence forever.

13 Blessed be Our God, the God of Israel,
   forever and ever!
   Amen, amen!

book II

42-43*

For the conductor
A teaching psalm by the disciples of Qorach

1. Like a stag, a doe, longing for streams of cool water,
     my whole being longs for you, my God.
2. My soul aches with thirst for God, for a god that lives!
     When can I go and see God face to face?
3. My only food, day or night, is my tears;
     they recriminate me:
   "Where is your God?" they say.

4. These things I remember
     as I pour out my soul like water—
   how I'd go with the crowds
     and lead them into God's house,
   amid cries of gladness and thanksgiving,
     drunk with the dance of celebration.

5. *"Why so dispirited?" I ask myself.*
     "Why so churned up inside? Hope in God!"
   I know I'll praise God once again,
     for you are my Deliverance;
     you are my God.

6. This is why my heart despairs:
     I remember other days with you,
   in the land of Jordan, on Mount Hermon
     and the Hill of Mizar.
7. The primeval Deep is echoing
     in the sound of your waterfalls;

---

* Psalms 42 and 43 were originally a single poem.

your torrents rage and break over me,
    overwhelming me.
8   Every day, Adonai, you ordain your love toward me,
    and during the night you bring me your song.
In my prayers to the God of my life,
9   I say to God, my rock:
"Why have you forgotten me?
    Why do you keep me in mourning,
    oppressed by an unseen enemy?"
10 My bones are shattered by their words,
    foes taunt me constantly:
    "Where is your God?" they say.

11 *"Why so dispirited?" I ask myself.*
    "Why so churned up inside? Hope in God!"
I know I'll praise God once again,
    for you are my Deliverance;
    you are my God.

43:1 Vindicate me, God!
    Plead my cause before unjust judges!
Rescue me from a lying, deceitful accuser.
2   For you, O God, are my stronghold, my defense.
Why have you forgotten me?
    Why do you keep me in mourning,
    oppressed by an unseen enemy?

3   Send forth your light and your truth—
    let them guide me,
let them bring me to your holy mountain,
    to your dwelling place.
4   Then at last I'll go up again
    to the altar of God,
    the God of my joy and delight.
My harp and lyre will sing your praise once again,
    O God, my God.

5   *"Why so dispirited?" I ask myself.*
    "Why so churned up inside? Hope in God!"
I know I'll praise God once again,
    for you are my Deliverance;
    you are my God.

44

For the conductor
By the disciples of Qorach
A teaching psalm

1 O God, we heard with our own ears—
     our ancestors told us
   all the things you did in their days,
     in days of old.
2 Your hand drove the nations out
     and planted them instead.
   You crushed the peoples,
     yet made our forebears take root.
3 It was not our ancestors' swords that won them the land,
     nor their arm that gave them the victory,
   but your mighty hand
     and your arm,
   the light of your presence—
     and your love for them.

4 You are my ruler, my God!
     At your bidding the children of Israel are victorious.
5 Through you we push back our enemies,
     in your Name we march over our adversaries.
6 I won't trust in my bow,
     nor will my sword win me the victory;
7 but it is you who makes us victorious over our enemies
     and puts our foes to shame.
8 We boast about you all day long, O God,
     and will praise your Name forever.
                —— Selah ——

9 But now you've rejected and chastened us
     and no longer lead our armies into battle.
10 You made us retreat before our enemy,
     and our foes pillage freely.
11 You've abandoned us to be butchered like sheep,
     and scattered us among the nations.

12 You have sold your people off for a pittance
     and did not consider them of much value.
13 You have made us the mockery of our neighbors,
     the scorn and contempt of those around us.
14 You've made us an example, a warning for the nations,
     and an object of ridicule among the peoples.

15 I brood on my disgrace all day long,
     and the shame on my face is exposed to all,
16 as my enemies assail me with taunts and abuse
     and take their revenge on me.
17 Every possible indignation has befallen us
     even though we didn't forget you
     or betray your Covenant;
18 we have not gone back on our word,
     nor did our feet stray from your path.
19 Yet you've broken us and thrust us into a pit of jackals,
     and covered us with a death pall.
20 If we had forgotten the Name of our God,
     or spread our hands in prayer to a god we've never known,
21 wouldn't you have discovered it, Adonai,
     since you know the hidden recesses of our heart?
22 Because of you we face a bloodbath all day long,
     and are treated as sheep for slaughter.

23 Wake up! Why do you sleep, Adonai?
     Rouse yourself! Don't reject us forever!
24 Why do you turn your face from us
     and ignore our misery and oppression?
25 We're falling down to the dust,
     we're lying in the dirt.
26 Arise and come to our help!
     Ransom us in your great love!

45

For the conductor
To the tune of "Lilies"
A teaching psalm by the disciples of Qorach
A wedding song

1   My heart is stirred with this sweet melody;
        I serenade you with my verse, my leader:
        my tongue is like the pen of a skillful writer.

2   Over all the earth, you are the most stately in manner,
        and the most charming of speakers,
        because God has blessed you forever.

3   Gird your sword upon your thigh, my champion,
        triumph by your splendor
        and subdue by your grandeur!

4   In your majesty ride forth
        for the cause of truth and the defense of the just.
        Let your right hand proclaim
        your awesome deeds!

5   Your arrows are sharp;
        they pierce the hearts of your enemies
        and make the nations cower before you.

6   For God has enthroned you forever and ever,
        and your royal scepter is a rod of justice.

7   And because you love justice and hate corruption,
        God, your God, has set you above your companions
        and anointed you with the oil of gladness.

8   Your robes are all fragrant with myrrh, aloes and cassia.
        Stringed instruments entertain you in ivory palaces.

9   Daughters of dignitaries are in your retinue,
        and at your right hand stands the queen in gold from Ophir.

10 Listen, my daughter! Give this your full attention:
        forget your country and your ancestral home,

11 for the ruler is enthralled by your beauty;
        give honor as you would to your sovereign.

12 A Tyrian robe is among your gifts,
        and great dignitaries will court your favor with jewels.

13 You, my daughter, will be gloriously dressed
        in a gown woven with gold.

14 Adorned in splendid robes you make your way to the ruler,
    and arrive with your friends as your attendants.
15 With joy and gladness you go in procession
    as you enter the palace of the ruler.

16 Your children will take the place of your ancestors,
    and you'll make them rulers throughout all the earth.
17 And I will make your name remembered
    from one generation to another,
  so that the nations will praise you
    forever and ever.

46

For the conductor
By the disciples of Qorach
A song for soprano voices

1 God is our refuge and our strength,
    who from of old has helped us in our distress.
2 Therefore we fear nothing—
    even if the earth should open up in front of us
    and mountains plunge into the depths of the sea,
3 even if the earth's waters rage and foam
    and the mountains tumble with its heaving.

4 There's a river whose streams gladden the city of God,
    the holy dwelling of the Most High.
5 God is in its midst;
    it will never fall—
    God will help it at daybreak.
6 Though nations are in turmoil and empires crumble,
    God's voice resounds, and it melts the earth.

7 *Adonai Sabaoth is with us—*
    our stronghold is the God of Israel!

8 Come, see what Our God has done—
    God makes the earth bounteous!

9   God has put an end to war,
         from one end of the earth to the other,
     breaking bows, splintering spears,
         and setting chariots on fire.
10   "Be still, and know that I am God!
         I will be exalted among the nations;
         I will be exalted upon the earth."

11   *Adonai Sabaoth is with us;*
         our stronghold is the God of Israel!

47

For the conductor
By the disciples of Qorach
A psalm

1   People everywhere—clap your hands!
         Shout to God with a joyful voice!
2   For Our God Most High is awe-inspiring,
         the great Ruler over the whole earth.
3   God subdues peoples for us,
         and puts the nations under our feet.
4   God chooses our inheritance for us,
         the pride of Leah, Rachel and Jacob,
         the object of God's love.
5   God ascended the throne with a shout,
         with trumpet blasts!
6   Sing praise to God, sing praise!
         sing praise to our Ruler, sing praise!
7   For God rules over all the earth—
         sing praise and understand!
8   God rules over the nations;
         God sits on the throne of holiness.
9   World leaders are gathered,
         and so are the people of Sarah and Abraham's God,
     for Our God reigns over all the earth,
         and is exalted above all.

A song of praise
By the disciples of Qorach

1 How great is Adonai, how worthy of praise
in the city of Our God, on God's holy mountain—
2 beautiful and lofty, the joy of all the earth!
Mount Zion, "the heart of the earth,"
is the city of the great Ruler.
3 And for all its citadels,
God is Zion's true fortress.

4 Look—the rulers joined forces
and made their attack.
5 But when they saw Zion,
they were terrified and fled,
6 quaking in their boots,
screaming in pain like a woman in labor.
7 Just as we had heard reports
that you smashed the ships of Tarshish
with a strong east wind,
8 so we now see with our own eyes
in the city of Adonai Sabaoth,
in the city of our God:
it is God who makes Zion secure forever.
—— *Selah* ——

9 O God, we meditate on your love
within your Temple.
10 As your Name reaches the ends of the earth, O God,
so does your praise;
justice fills your right hand.
11 Mount Zion rejoices,
and the villages of Judah celebrate
because of your judgments.
12 Walk throughout Zion—make the rounds
and count the towers!
13 Ponder its ramparts, examine its citadels,
so that you can tell a future generation
14 that God is our God, forever and ever—
and God will guide us even to our last day.

49

For the conductor
By the disciples of Qorach
A psalm of praise

1 Hear this, everyone!
  Listen, all who live on the earth—
2 both women and men,
  rich and poor alike!
3 My mouth will speak wisdom,
  and my heart will utter knowledge.
4 I'll sing you a riddle,
  and with my harp I'll explain its meaning:

5 Why should I be afraid in times of danger,
  or when I'm surrounded by those who lie and deceive?
6 They trust only in their money,
  and boast of nothing but their great wealth.
7 Yet even they cannot redeem another person—
  no one can pay God the ransom for someone else,
8 because the payment for a life is too great.
  What they can pay will never be enough
9 to keep them from the grave,
  to let them live forever.
10 They see that even the wise die,
  as do the foolish and stupid.
  They all perish
  and leave their riches to others.
11 Their graves will be their homes forever;
  there they'll live from one generation to the next,
  even though they once had lands of their own.
12 Their prosperity cannot keep them from death;
  they'll die just like any animal.
13 This is the fate of those who trust in themselves,
  and of their like-minded followers:
14 they are doomed to die like sheep,
  and death will be their shepherd.
  The righteous will rule over them in the morning,
  as their bodies decay in the land of the dead,
  far away from their mansions.

15 But God will redeem me,
    and will pluck me out of Death's control.

16 So don't be envious when people become rich,
    when they make their homes even grander—
17 because they can't take it with them when they die;
    their splendor will not join them in the grave.
18 Even though they're successful in this life,
    and are praised because they prosper,
19 they'll join all their ancestors in death,
    where the darkness lasts forever.
20 Those who are prosperous but without understanding
    will die just like any animal.

50

1 Adonai, Our God,
    speaks and summons the earth
from the rising of the sun
    to its setting.
2 Out of Zion, the perfection of beauty,
    God shines forth.
3 Our God comes, and won't be silent:
    a devouring fire goes before God,
    while storms rage all around.
4 God summons heaven and earth
    to the trial of God's people:
5 "Gather to me my faithful ones,
    who make their covenant with me by sacrifice!"
6 The heavens affirm God's justice
    because it is God who is the judge!
            —— Selah ——

7 "Hear, O my people, and I will speak!
    Hear, O Israel, and I will testify against you!
    I am God—your God.
8 I don't fault you for your sacrifices—
    on the contrary, your burnt offerings are always before me.

⁹ It's just that I don't need oxen from your stall,
    or goats from your folds,
¹⁰ since every beast of the forest is mine already;
    I have cattle on a thousand hills!
¹¹ I know every bird in the mountains,
    and all that moves in the field is mine.
¹² If I were hungry, I wouldn't tell you,
    for the world and all that is in it is mine.
¹³ Do I eat the flesh of oxen,
    or drink the blood of goats?
¹⁴ Offer me a sacrifice of thanksgiving instead,
    and fulfill the vow you make to me!
¹⁵ Then call upon me in the day of trouble—
    I will deliver you, and you will honor me."

¹⁶ But to the corrupt God says:
    "What right have you to recite my statutes
      or take my covenant on your lips?
¹⁷ For you hate discipline,
    and you throw away my words as if they were trash.
¹⁸ If you see a thief, you join in the thieving;
    and you cheat alongside other adulterers.
¹⁹ You give your mouth free reign for evil,
    and your tongue frames deceit.
²⁰ You sit and speak against your sisters and brothers,
    and you slander your own siblings.
²¹ I didn't say a word while you did those things—
    you thought that I was just like you.
    But now I rebuke you
      and accuse you to your face.
²² So consider this, you who forget me—
    or I'll tear you to pieces with no hope of rescue!
²³ Those who bring thanksgiving as their sacrifice
    honor me and prepare my road.
    To these I will reveal my salvation."

51

For the conductor
A psalm of David
Written when the prophet Nathan came to him
after David had relations with Bathsheba

1 O God, have mercy on me!
  Because of your love and your great compassion,
    wipe away my faults;
2 wash me clean of my guilt,
    purify me of my sin.
3 For I am aware of my faults,
    and have my sin constantly in mind.
4 I sinned against you alone,
    and did what is evil in your sight.
  You are just when you pass sentence on me,
    blameless when you give judgment.

5 I was born in sin,
    conceived in sin—
6 yet you want truth to live in my innermost being.
    Teach me your wisdom!
7 Purify me with hyssop until I am clean;
    wash me until I am purer than new-fallen snow.
8 Instill some joy and gladness into me,
    let the bones you have crushed rejoice again.
9 Turn your face from my sins,
    and wipe out all my guilt.

10 O God, create a clean heart in me,
    put into me a new and steadfast spirit;
11 do not banish me from your presence,
    do not deprive me of your holy Spirit!
12 Be my savior again, renew my joy,
    keep my spirit steady and willing;
13 and I will teach transgressors your ways,
    and sinners will return to you.

14 Save me from bloodshed, O God, God of my salvation—
    and my tongue will acclaim your justice.
15 Open my lips, Adonai,
    and my mouth will declare your praise.

16 Sacrifice gives you no pleasure;
    were I to present a burnt offering,
    you would not have it.
17 My sacrifice, O God, is a broken spirit;
    you will not scorn this crushed and broken heart.

18 Make Zion prosper through your favor,
    and rebuild the walls of Jerusalem.
19 Then there will be proper sacrifice to please you—
    burnt offerings and whole oblations,
    and young bulls to be offered on your altar.

52

For the conductor
A teaching psalm by David
Written when Doeg the Edomite went to Saul and said,
"David has gone to Ahimelech's house"

1 How can you boast
    about how corrupt you are, you tyrant?
Even against God's beloved
2   you forge wild lies all day long—
your slanderous tongue
    is sharp as a razor!
3 You love evil, not good;
    falsehood, not truth-telling.
      —— *Selah* ——
4 You enjoy cruel gossip
    and slanderous talk.
5 So God will pull you down to the ground forever,
    sweep you away, leave you ruined and homeless
    and uprooted from the land of the living!
6 The righteous will look on, awestruck,
    and they will laugh at your plight.
7 "This is the one," they'll say,
    "who didn't seek refuge in God,
but trusted in great wealth
    and grew strong by destroying others."

8 I am an olive tree flourishing in God's house,
       for I trust in God's love forever and ever.
9 I will praise you forever for what you have done;
       among your faithful I will put my trust in your Name,
       for it is good.

For the conductor
About sickness
A teaching psalm by David

1 Fools say in their hearts,
       "There is no God."
    They are corrupt, and do despicable wrongs—
       there is none who does good.
2 God looks down from heaven
       on all of humankind,
    to see whether any
       are wise or seek God.
3 But they've all turned away;
       they all became corrupt together.
    None of them does good—
       not a single one.
4 Will they never learn, these evildoers
       who devour my people like bread,
       and never call upon God?
5 There they are, consumed with fear—
       when there was never anything to fear!
    For God scattered the bones of those who attacked you, Israel—
       you put them to shame,
       for God had rejected them.

6 Who will come from Zion
       to bring the deliverance of Israel?
    When God's people are brought back from captivity,
       the descendants of Leah, Rachel and Jacob will rejoice;
       the children of Israel will be glad.

To the conductor: for strings
A teaching psalm by David
Written when the Ziphites went to Saul and said,
"David is hidden among us!"

1 O God, save me by the power of your Name,
　　defend me by your might!

2 God, hear my prayer,
　　listen to the words of my mouth.

3 Strangers attack me,
　　ruthless scoundrels seek my life;
　　they don't give God a single thought.
　　　　　—— *Selah* ——

4 For you are my helper,
　　the One who sustains my life.

5 May their own malice recoil on my slanderers;
　　silence them with your truth.

6 I will offer you a willing sacrifice
　　and praise your Name, Adonai, for it is good.

7 You have rescued me from every trouble;
　　I have seen my enemies' downfall with my own eyes.

To the conductor: for strings
A teaching psalm by David

1 O God, hear my prayer—
     don't ignore my pleas!
2 Hear me! Answer me!
     My mind is tortured and I am distraught
3 at the sound of my enemies,
     at their vicious oppression.
   They engulf me with their treachery
     and assault me in anger.
4 My heart is tortured inside me;
     terrors of death assail me.
5 Fear and trembling invade me;
     horror overwhelms me.

6 So I said, "If only I had the wings of a dove!
     Then I'd fly away and find rest.
7 Yes, I'd fly far away,
     and find rest in the desert.
                —— *Selah* ——
8 I'd hurry to my place of refuge,
     far from this raging wind and storm."

9 Confound them, Adonai, confuse their speech,
     for I see nothing but violence and strife in the city.
10 Day and night they prowl its borders;
     malice and trouble roam its streets.
11 Violence fills the city,
     fraud and deceit never leave its marketplace.

12 For it is not an enemy who reviles me—
     I could bear that!
   It is not a foe who taunts me—
     or I could hide and be safe.
13 No, it is you, my other self,
     my companion, my bosom friend!—
14 we who together held sweet communion;
     we walked to God's house amid the festive throng!

¹⁵ Let Destruction seize them without warning!
  Let Sheol swallow them alive!
For Corruption will make its home with them
  wherever they are.
¹⁶ As for me, I will call on God
  and God will save me.
¹⁷ Evening, morning and noon
  I lament and groan
  and my Liberator hears my voice.
¹⁸ God ransoms me whole
  from those who wage war against me,
  though many oppose me.
¹⁹ God will hear me and overthrow them—
  the One who has reigned from the beginning—
    —— *Selah* ——
because they will never change:
  they have no reverence for God.

²⁰ And you, my former friend—
  you even attack your soulmates
  and violate your covenant with them.
²¹ Your talk is as smooth as butter,
  but in your heart there is war;
your words are more soothing than oil,
  yet they conceal the drawn sword.

²² Cast your burden on God,
  who will sustain you,
  and will never allow the righteous to be overthrown.
²³ But God will bring your enemies down
  to the pit of destruction;
those murderous deceivers will not live out half their days.
  Adonai, I will trust in you!

To the conductor: to the tune of "A Dove on the Far Oaks"
By David
A poem written when the Philistines seized him in Gath

1 O God, have mercy on me, for the enemy persecutes me,
      my assailants harass me all day long.
2 All day long my slanderers persecute me;
      countless are those who assail me, Exalted One.

3 *When I am afraid,*
      I will trust in you.
4 *In you I will shout defiance!*
      In you I will trust and let go of my fear—
      what can mortals do to me?

5 All day long they twist my words,
      all their thoughts are hostile.
6 They plot, they wait in ambush,
      they watch my every move,
      eager to take my life.
7 Don't let them escape!
      O God, in your anger bring ruin to the nations.
8 You write down all my laments,
      and store every tear in your wineskin—
      have you counted each one?
9 Then my enemies will turn back
      on the day I call upon you;
10 this I know—
      that God is on my side.

   In you I will shout defiance!
11   *In you I will trust and let go of my fear—*
      what can mortals do to me?

12 I have bound myself with vows to you, O God,
      and will redeem them with thank-offerings;
13 for you have rescued me from death
      and kept my feet from stumbling,
   to walk in your presence,
      in the light of life.

To the conductor: to the tune of "Do Not Destroy"
By David
A poem, written when he ran from Saul and hid in a cave

1 Have mercy on me, O God, have mercy on me!
      In you my soul takes shelter;
   I take shelter in the shadow of your wings
      until the destroying storm is over.
2 I call on God the Most High,
      on God who has done everything for me,
3 to send help from heaven to save me,
      to stop them from persecuting me.
               —— *Selah* ——
   O God, send me your love
      and your faithfulness.
4 I'm surrounded by lions
      greedy for human prey,
   their teeth are spears and arrows,
      their tongue a sharp sword.
5 Rise high above the heavens, O God,
      and let your glory cover the earth!
6 They laid a net where I was walking
      when I was bowed with care;
   they dug a pit for me
      but fell into it themselves.
               —— *Selah* ——

7 My heart is ready, O God,
      my heart is ready;
   I will sing and play for you.
8 Awake, my muse!
      Awake, lyre and harp!
   I will awaken the dawn!
9 I will thank you among the peoples, Adonai,
      and sing of you among the nations;
10 your love is high as heaven,
      your faithfulness reaches to the skies.
11 Rise high above the heavens, O God,
      let your glory cover the earth!

To the conductor: to the tune of "Do Not Destroy"
By David
A poem

1 Do you really make just decisions, you leaders?
  Do you judge everyone fairly?
2 No! You think only of the injustice you will do;
  you commit crimes of violence in the land.
3 You've done wrong all your lives,
  and lied from the day you were born.
4 You are full of poison, like snakes;
  you stop up your ears, like a deaf cobra
5 that doesn't hear the voice of the snake charmer
  or the incantation of the fakir.

6 Break their teeth, Adonai!
  Tear out the fangs of these fierce lions!
7 Let them disappear like water draining away;
  Let them be crushed like weeds on the path.
8 Let them be like snails that dissolve into slime;
  let them be like a baby born dead
  that never sees the light.
9 Before these thorns can grow into brambles
  they'll be swept away
  whether they are green or dry.
10 The just will be glad when they see the corrupt punished;
  they will wade through the blood of the wicked.
11 People will say, "The just really are rewarded;
  there is indeed a God who judges the world!"

To the conductor: to the tune of "Do Not Destroy"
By David
A poem written when Saul sent guards to
watch David's house and try to kill him

1 Rescue me from my enemies, my God!
    Protect me from those who attack me!
2 Rescue me from those who love violence,
    and save me from this bloodthirsty gang!
3 Look! They lie in wait for my life;
    the powerful conspire against me
for no reason at all—
    I didn't do anything wrong, Adonai!
4 Though I committed no sin, they rush to take their stand.
    Awake, come to my aid and see!
5 You, Our God, God of Hosts, Israel's God—
    rise up and punish the nations;
    show no mercy to these evil traitors!
           —— *Selah* ——

6 Each evening they come back like dogs;
    they howl and roam the city.
[They prowl in search of food,
    they snarl till they've had their fill.] *

7 See what they spew from their mouths—
    their lips are filled with words that cut like a sword.
    "For who," they say, "will hear us?"
8 But you, Adonai, will laugh at them—
    you scoff at all the nations.

9 O my strength, I watch for you,
    for you, O God, are my stronghold.
10 The God who loves me
    will go before me;
God will let me gloat
    over the ones who slander me now.

---

* This part of the verse is found in the Greek version of the text, but is missing from the standard
Hebrew version.

11   O God, kill them, lest my people be seduced!
      By your power, scatter them and lay them low—
      you who are our shield, Adonai!
12   For the sins of their mouths and their lips,
      for the curses and lies that they speak,
      let them be caught in their pride.
13   Destroy them in your anger!
      Destroy them until they are no more!
    Then all will know that God rules in Israel
      and to the ends of the earth.
          —— *Selah* ——

14   Each evening they come back like dogs.
      They howl and roam the city,
15   they prowl in search of food,
      they snarl till they have had their fill.

16   As for me, I will sing of your strength
      and each morning acclaim your love;
    for you have been my stronghold,
      a refuge in the day of my distress.
17   O God my strength,
      it is you that I praise,
    for you, O God, are my stronghold—
      the God who loves.

60

To the conductor: To the tune of "The Lily of the Covenant"
A poem of David, for teaching
Written when he fought the Arameans of Mesopotamia and Syria, when
Joab returned and killed twelve thousand Edomites in the Valley of Salt

1 O God, you have rejected us
   and broken our defenses.
   You have been angry;
      restore us!
2 You have rocked the land and split it open;
   now repair the cracks that your earthquakes are causing!
3 You have made your people feel hardship,
   and given us stupefying wine.
4 Now raise a banner for those who revere you
   to which they may flee, out of bowshot,
5 that your loved ones may escape;
   help us by your mighty hand and answer us!

6 God promised in the sanctuary:
   "In triumph I will divide up Shechem,
      and measure off the Succoth Valley.
7 Gilead is mine,
      and so is Manasseh;
   Ephraim is the helmet for my head,
      and Judah is my scepter;
8 Moab will serve as my washbowl,
      upon Edom I will set my shoes,
   and over Philistia
      I will shout my triumph!"

9 Who will bring me into the fortified city?
   Who will lead me to Edom?
10 Isn't it you who have rejected us, O God,
    and no longer go forth with our armies?
11 Give us aid against the enemy,
    for all other help is worthless.
12 With God we will triumph;
    God will trample our enemies.

61

To the conductor: for strings
By David

1 O God, hear my cry;
   listen to my prayer!
2 From the end of the earth I call to you,
   and now my heart grows weak.
 Set me on a rock
   that is higher than I.
3 For you have been my shelter,
   a tower of strength when I am in danger.
4 In your tent I will make my home forever,
   and take shelter under the cover of your wings.
—— *Selah* ——

5 For you've heard my vows, O God,
   and given me the inheritance
   reserved for those who revere your Name.
6 To my life as a ruler, add one day, then another,
   then year upon year and generation upon generation.
7 Let me rule in God's presence forever,
   and let love and faithfulness be my protectors.
8 Then I will sing praises forever to your Name
   as I fulfill my vows day after day.

To the conductor: for Jeduthun
A psalm of David

1 In God alone my soul finds rest,
    for my deliverance comes from God,
2 who alone is my rock, my salvation, my fortress:
    I will never be shaken.

3 How long will you besiege me
    as though I were a crumbling wall
    or a tottering fence?
4 They connive to push me off a cliff,
    they delight in telling lies.
With their mouths they utter blessing,
    but in their hearts they curse.
      —— *Selah* ——

5 In God alone my soul finds rest,
    for my deliverance comes from God,
6 who alone is my rock, my salvation, my fortress:
    I will never be shaken.

7 Only in God—my deliverance, my glory—
    my refuge is God.
8 Trust in God always, my people;
    pour out your hearts before God our refuge.
9 Humankind is but a breath,
    mortals are just an illusion.
Put them on the scales and the balance is thrown off:
    they weigh less than a breath.
10 Do not trust in extortion,
    or put false hopes in stolen goods;
do not set your heart on riches
    even when they increase.

11 For God has said only one thing,
    only two do I know:
that to God alone belongs power,
12   and that you, Adonai, are loving—
you repay all people
    according to their deeds.

63

1 Adonai, my God,
    you are the One I seek.
My soul thirsts for you,
    my body longs for you
in this dry and weary land
    where there is no water.
2 So I look to you in the sanctuary
    to see your power and glory;
3 because your love is better than life,
    my lips will glorify you.

4 And so I bless you while I live;
    in your Name I lift up my hands.
5 My soul will be sated as with a sumptuous feast,
    and with euphoric cries I will praise you.
6 I remember you when I'm in bed;
    through sleepless nights I meditate on you,
7 because you are my help,
    and in the shadow of your wings I sing for joy.
8 My soul clings to you;
    your mighty hand upholds me.

9 But those who seek my life will be destroyed,
    they'll be cast into the bowels of the earth;
10 they will be delivered over to the sword,
    and will become food for jackals.
11 But I will rejoice in God,
    everyone who swears by God will rejoice,
but the mouths of those who tell lies
    will be silenced.

1 O God, hear the voice of my lament!
     Keep me safe from the threats of the enemy.
2 Hide me from that vicious gang,
     from that mob of evildoers
3 who sharpen their tongues like swords
     and wing their cruel words like arrows
4 to ambush the innocent like a sniper,
     shooting without warning, themselves unseen.
5 They encourage each other in their evil plans
     and brag about how they hide their snares,
     secure that no one will see them;
6 they plot their secret injustices with skill and cunning,
     with evil purpose and deep design.

7 But God's arrows hit their mark,
     and their downfall will be sudden.
8 Their own mischievous tongues will be their undoing,
     and all who see them will recoil in horror.
9 All humankind will be afraid:
     "This is God's doing," they'll say,
     and they'll learn their lesson from what God has done.

10 But the just will rejoice and seek refuge in Our God;
     let the upright in heart give praise!

65

For the conductor
A psalm of David
A song

1   O God, to you we owe hymns of praise in Zion;
    to you our vows must be fulfilled,
2   you who hear our prayers
    and before whom all flesh must stand.
3   When we are overcome by our sins,
    you provide the atonement for them.
4   Happy are those you choose, those you draw near
    to dwell in your courts!
    We are filled with the blessings of your house,
    the holy things of your Temple!

5   With powerful deeds of justice
    you answer us, God our Deliverer,
    in whom all the ends of the earth
    and the farthest seas put their trust.
6   You set the mountains in place by your power,
    having armed yourself with might.
7   You still the roaring of the seas,
    the roaring of the waves, and the tumult of the peoples.
8   And those who dwell at the ends of the earth
    stand in awe of your marvels;
    you make the sunrise and sunset shout for joy!
9   You nourish and water the land—
    greatly you have enriched it.
    The streams of God are full of water;
    you provide us with grain as you ordained.
10 Thus have you prepared the land:
    drenching its furrows,
    breaking up its clods, softening it with showers,
    blessing its yield.
11 You have crowned the year with your bounty
    and your paths overflow with a rich harvest;
12 the untilled meadows overflow with abundance,
    and rejoicing clothes the hills.
13 The fields are covered with flocks
    and the valleys are blanketed with grain.
    They shout and sing for joy!

1 Shout to God,
    all the earth!
2 Sing the glory of God's Name—
    give glorious praise!
3 Say to God,
    "How awesome are your deeds!
    Your enemies cower before your great strength!
4 The whole earth worships you
    and sings praises to you—
    all creation praises your Name!"
        —— *Selah* ——

5 Come and see the works of God—
    God's deeds on our behalf are wondrous.
6 God turned the sea into dry land;
    and people passed through the river on foot.
There we rejoiced in God,
7   whose reign of power lasts forever,
whose eyes keep watch on the nations
    so that the rebellious don't exalt themselves before God.

8 Bless our God, all you peoples,
    let the sound of God's praise be heard!
9 God has kept us among the living,
    and has not let our feet slip.
10 For you have tested us, O God—
    you have refined us as silver is refined.
11 You put us in prisons
    and laid burdens on our backs;
12 you let people ride over our heads;
    we went through fire and through water—
    and you brought us to a place of abundance and space.

13 I will come to your house with burnt offerings;
    I will pay my vows to you,
14 the ones my lips uttered
    and my mouth promised when I was in trouble.

¹⁵ I will present you burnt offerings of fatlings,
   with the smoke of burning rams;
   I will make an offering of bulls and goats.
           —— *Selah* ——
¹⁶ Come and hear, all who revere God,
   and I will tell what the Holy One has done for me.
¹⁷ I cried aloud to God,
   and praise was on my tongue.
¹⁸ If I had nursed evil in my heart,
   God would not have listened.
¹⁹ But God did listen,
   and heeded the voice of my prayer.
²⁰ Blessed be God,
   who has not rejected my prayer
   or stopped loving me!

67

To the conductor: for strings
A song of praise

¹ O God, show us kindness and bless us,
   and make your face smile on us!
           —— *Selah* ——
² For then the earth will acknowledge your ways,
   and all the nations will know of your power to save.
³ Let the peoples praise you, O God,
   let all the peoples praise you!
⁴ Let the nations shout and sing for joy,
   for you dispense true justice to the world—
   you guide the nations of the earth!
⁵ Let the peoples shout and sing for joy,
   let all the peoples praise you!
⁶ The land has given its harvest:
   God, our God, has blessed us.
⁷ May God bless us, and may God be revered
   even to the ends of the earth!

To the conductor
By David
A song of praise

1   Arise, O God, and scatter your enemies!
        Make your enemies flee before you!
2   As smoke disappears in the air, so make them disappear!
        As wax melts in fire, let the violent vanish before you!
3   But let the righteous be joyful!
        Let them exult before God,
        let them be jubilant with joy!
4   Sing praise to the Rider of the Clouds
        whose Name is Adonai!
        Exult before God!
5   A parent to the orphan
        and protector of the defenseless
        is our God, who dwells in holiness!
6   God creates families for those who are alone,
        and leads captives to freedom;
        but the rebellious dwell in a parched land.

7   O God, when you went forth before your people,
        when you marched through the wilderness,
                —— *Selah* ——
8   the earth quaked, the heavens poured down rain
        before you, the One of Sinai—
        before you, the God of Israel.
9   You gave rain in abundance, O God,
        you restored the land—our inheritance—when it languished;
10 your tribe found a dwelling in it,
        in your goodness, O God, you provided for the needy.

11 Adonai gave the command,
        and the women who carried the good news
        were a great throng:
12 "The rulers and their armies,
        they flee, they flee!
13 And women who have no standing
        are dividing the spoil;

and even for those of you who sleep in the sheepfolds,
  there are wings of a dove—with pinions of fine gold—
  in a silver sheath!
14 When Shaddai scattered the rulers in Zalmon,
  it looked like a snowstorm had swept through!"

15 Mountain of majesty, mountain of Bashan!
  Mountain of tall peaks, mountain of Bashan!
16 Why look with envy, you many-peaked mountain,
  toward the mount where God chose to reign,
  where Adonai will dwell forever?
17 With God's Chariot—
  and with twenty thousand, and thousands more—
  Adonai came from Sinai into the sanctuary.
18 When you ascended the high mount,
  you led captives in your train
and received tribute
  from those you conquered—
even from those who rebel
  against the Most High God who lives there.

19 Blessed be Our God, who supports us day by day—
  God alone is our Savior!
    —— *Selah* ——
20 Our God is a God of salvation,
  since to Adonai we owe our escape from death.
21 God will strike down the rulers of your enemies,
  their leaders who continue in their guilty ways.
22 God said,
  "I who stifled the Serpent
  and muzzled the Deep Sea
23 will let you walk away unscathed
  and leave your enemies to the dogs."

24 Your solemn processions are coming into view now, O God—
  the processions of my God, my Ruler,
  have come into the sanctuary—
25 the singers in front, then the musicians,
  and all around them the young people playing tambourines.
26 "Bless God in your great congregation," they sing,
  "you who are Israel's fountain!"

27 Then comes little Benjamin, leading the rest:
    the royalty of Judah in their throng,
    then the royalty of Zebulun and of Naphtali.

28 Summon your power, O God;
    show the strength that you have shown to us before, O God!
29 Because of your Temple at Jerusalem,
    rulers bring you gifts.
30 Rebuke the Beast of the Reeds!
    It is a herd of bulls inciting its calves—the nations—
    to stampede over people for lust of silver.
God will scatter the nations whose lust creates war,
31   and Egypt's wealthy will come bearing tribute,
    Cush will hurry to God with gifts in hand.

32 Sing to God, all the earth's realms!
    Sing praises to Adonai!
      —— *Selah* ——
33 Sing to the Rider of the ancient skies,
    who thunders forth with a powerful voice!
34 Proclaim the power of God,
    whose majesty is over Israel,
    in the skies!
35 O God, how awesome you are in your sanctuary!
    The God of Israel gives power and strength to the people.
Blessed be God!

69

To the conductor: to the tune of "Lilies"
By David

1 O God, save me,
  for the waters are up to my neck!
2 I'm sinking into a deep swamp
  and can't find a foothold!
  I'm in very deep water,
  and its torrents are overwhelming me.
3 I'm exhausted from crying,
  my throat is raw;
  and my sight is blurring
  from looking for my God.
4 Those who hate me for no reason
  outnumber the hairs of my head.
  So many would destroy me,
  so many accuse me without cause,
  and force me to restore
  what I didn't steal!

5 O God, you know how foolish I've been,
  and my faults are not hidden from you.
6 Don't let those who look to you be disappointed because of me,
  Sovereign God of Hosts!
  Don't let those who seek you be ashamed because of me,
  O God of Israel,
7 since it is for your sake that I bear insult,
  that shame covers my face.
8 I've become an outcast in my own family,
  a stranger to my mother's children—
9 and because I am consumed with zeal for your House,
  the insults of those who ridicule you
  fall upon me.
10 When I weep and fast,
  I receive nothing but abuse.
11 When I dress in sackcloth,
  I am called a buffoon.
12 They sit at the gate gossiping about me,
  and drunks make me the butt of their songs.

13 But I pray to you, Adonai,
     for the time of your favor, O God!
   In your great love, answer me!
     With you is sure deliverance!
14 Rescue me from the quicksand—
     don't let me sink!
   Let me be rescued from my enemies,
     and from the watery depths.
15 Don't let the raging flood engulf me,
     don't let the abyss swallow me up,
     or the pit close its mouth over me.
16 Answer me, Adonai, for your love is wonderful!
     In your great mercy, turn toward me.
17 Don't hide your face from your faithful one;
     I am in trouble—hurry and answer me!
18 Come and ransom my life;
     as an answer to my enemies, redeem me.

19 You know my torment, my shame and my dishonor;
     You see how my enemies treat me.
20 My heart aches from their insults and I am helpless;
     I look for sympathy, but to no avail;
     for comforters, but find none.
21 Instead, they poisoned my food,
     and for my thirst they gave me vinegar to drink.
22 May they be trapped by the table they set;
     may their own friends be caught in its snare!
23 May their eyes grow dim so that they cannot see,
     and their backs become increasingly feeble!
24 Pour out your wrath upon them;
     let the fury of your anger sweep them away!
25 Let their encampment become deserted;
     let their tents stand empty!
26 For they persecute the one you struck,
     and add insult to the pain of the one you wounded.
27 Charge them with crime upon crime,
     and don't let them share in your promise!
28 Erase their names from the Book of the Living,
     and don't record them among the just!

29 I am suffering and in pain—
     let your saving help protect me, God!

³⁰ Then I will praise your Name in song,
  and glorify you with thanksgiving.
³¹ This will please you more than oxen
  or bulls with their horns and hooves.
³² See and be glad, you who have nothing!
  You who seek God, take heart!
³³ For Our God hears the poor;
  God has not neglected those who are captives.
³⁴ Let heaven and earth praise God,
  the seas and all that moves in them!
³⁵ For God will free Zion
  and rebuild the cities of Judah,
and those who were expelled from the land
  will return at last.
³⁶ The descendants of God's faithful ones will inherit it,
  and those who love God's Name will inhabit it.

70

To the conductor
By David
A petition

¹ O God, save me!
  Adonai, help me, and hurry!
² Let those who seek my life
  be humiliated and dazed!
Let those who wish me harm
  flee in disgrace!
³ Those who jeer, "Aha! Aha!"—
  make them retreat, covered with shame!
⁴ Let all who seek you
  rejoice and be glad in you!
Let those who love your salvation
  forever say, "God is great!"
⁵ As for me, I am wretched and poor, my God—
  hurry to my side!
You are my rescuer, my help;
  Adonai, do not delay.

1 In you, Adonai, I take shelter—
    let me never be disappointed.
2 In your justice, rescue me, deliver me,
    turn your ear to me and save me!
3 Be mine, O mountain of strength!
    Send your decree—deliver me,
    for you are my rock, my fortress!
4 O God, rescue me from the hands of the violent,
    from the clutches of the thief and outlaw!

5 For you alone are my hope, Adonai my sovereign—
    I have trusted you since my youth.
6 I have relied on you from the womb;
    you sustained me from my mother's breast;
    to you I give constant praise.
7 I have become a target for many,
    but you are my firm refuge.
8 My mouth is filled with your praise,
    full of your splendor all day long.
9 Don't throw me away now that I am old,
    nor desert me now that my strength is failing.

10 For my enemies are spying on me,
    and those who are waiting for me to die
    are hatching conspiracies.
11 They say, "God has forsaken you!
    We will pursue you, then catch you—
    for there is no one to rescue you."
12 O God, don't be far from me!
    My God, come quickly and help me!
13 May those who slander me be utterly humiliated;
    let those who want to hurt me
    be covered with insult and disgrace.

14 As for me, I'll always have hope,
    and I will add to all your praises.
15 My lips will proclaim your deeds of justice and salvation
    all day long, even though they are innumerable.

¹⁶ O God, I will enter your mighty Temple
and there proclaim your justice.

¹⁷ You taught me when I was young,
and I am still proclaiming your marvels.
¹⁸ Now that I am old and gray,
O God, do not desert me;
let me live to tell the coming generation
about your strength and power.

¹⁹ Your justice, O God, is higher than the heavens.
You have done great things;
who is comparable to you?
²⁰ Though you have sent me much misery and hardship,
you will give me life again,
you will raise me up again
from the depths of the earth;
²¹ you'll increase my honor
and once again comfort me.

²² And so on the lyre I'll praise you,
my ever-faithful God;
I will play the harp in your honor,
Holy One of Israel.
²³ My lips will sing for joy while I play for you—
my whole being, which you have redeemed, will sing.
²⁴ And all day long, my tongue will speak of your beneficence—
how those who wanted to hurt me
were put to shame and humiliated!

1 O God, give your anointed one your judgment—
  and your justice.
2 Teach your chosen one to govern your people rightly
  and bring justice to the oppressed.
3 The mountains will bring the people peace
  and the hills justice!
4 Your anointed will defend the oppressed among the people,
  save the children of the poor,
  and crush the oppressor.
5 The reign of your anointed will endure
  as long as the sun and moon—
  throughout all generations.
6 The rule of the chosen one will be
  like rain coming down on the meadow,
  like showers watering the earth.
7 Justice will flower through the days, and profound peace,
  until the moon be no more.

8 Your anointed will rule from sea to sea,
  and from the Euphrates to the ends of the earth.
9 The desert tribes will bow before the throne
  and the enemies of your chosen one will lick the dust.
10 Tarshish and the Isles will offer gifts;
  Arabia and Sheba will bring tribute.
11 All rulers will pay homage,
  and all the nations will serve your anointed.
12 Your anointed will rescue the poor when they cry out,
  and the oppressed when there is no one to help them.
13 Your chosen one
  will take pity on the lowly and the poor,
  and will save their lives.
14 Your chosen one
  will rescue them all from violence and oppression,
  and will treat their blood as precious.

15 Long live the Anointed One!
   Bring a tribute of gold from Sheba!
   Let the ruler be prayed for continually,
   and blessed day after day!
16 Let there be an abundance of grain upon the earth—
   let it rustle on the mountaintops!
   Let the crops flourish like the forests of Lebanon;
   let them thrive like the grass of the fields.
17 May the name of your Anointed One endure forever,
   and continue as long as the sun.
   In your Chosen the nations of earth will be blessed,
   and they will bless the Anointed in return.

18 Blessed be Our God, the God of Israel,
   who alone does wondrous deeds!
19 And blessed forever be God's glorious Name;
   may the whole earth be filled with God's glory.
   Amen, amen!

20 Here end the prayers of David begot of Jesse.

book III

1 Israel, how good your God is
   to those who are single-hearted!

2 My feet had almost strayed—
   a little farther and I would have slipped,
3 for I had envied those who boast of their success
   and begrudged the prosperity of the corrupt.
4 They have no struggles,
   their bodies are healthy and strong;
5 they don't suffer as others do,
   they're not afflicted like the rest of humanity!
6 So pride is their badge of honor,
   violence is the robe that covers them;
7 their eyes gorge themselves on new luxuries,
   their taste for extravagance knows no limits.
8 They cynically attribute evil to God,
   and blame all oppression on the Most High;
9 they think their mouth speaks for heaven,
   that their tongue can dictate on earth.

10 This is why my people turn to them
   and lap up all they say,
11 asking, "How will God ever find out?
   Does the Most High know everything?
12 Look at them: these are the corrupt,
   yet they are well off and still getting richer!

13 What's the use of keeping my own heart pure,
  and washing my hands in innocence,
14 if God still plagues me all day long
  and brings new punishments every morning?"

15 Had I dared to say things like that,
  I would have been false to the circle of your disciples.
16 Instead, I sought to probe the problem of injustice,
  but found it nearly impossible—
17 until the day I entered God's sanctuary
  and saw the end in store for them.
18 They will certainly fall into Perdition;
  you urge them on to their own destruction
19 until they suddenly fall,
  done for, terrified to death.
20 Like waking up from a dream, Adonai,
  their fantasies will be dashed in an instant.

21 But since my heart was aggrieved,
  and I had a gut full of anger,
22 I became a stupid fool before you;
  I acted like a jackass, and I am sorry.
23 Even so, you were always at my side
  holding me by the hand.
24 Now lead me with your counsel
  and in the end, bring me into your glory.
25 I look to no one else in heaven,
  I delight in nothing else on earth.
26 My body and mind may fail
  and my heart may pine for love,
 but God is my heart's rock,
  and my portion forever.

27 So then: those who are far from you will be lost,
  and you will destroy those who break faith with you.
28 But as for me, my joy lies in being close to God.
  I have taken refuge in you, Adonai my Sovereign,
  proclaiming without end what you have done.

1   O God, why have you cast us off forever?
      Why does your anger smolder
      against the sheep of your pasture?
2   Remember the flock you made yours so long ago—
      the tribe you ransomed as your inheritance—
      and Mount Zion, where you dwelled.

3   Pick your way through these utter ruins,
      all this damage the enemy has done in the sanctuary.
4   Your foes roar triumphantly in your Temple;
      they have set up their tokens of victory.
5   They are like people coming up with axes
      to a thicket of trees—
6   and now with chisel and hammer
      they hack away at its carved paneling.
7   They set your sanctuary on fire,
      burned it to the ground,
      and profaned the place where your Name abides.
8   They said in their hearts,
      "Let's destroy them,
      and burn all the shrines of God in their land!"

9   We have been given no signs;
      there is no prophet now,
      and no one understands the evidence before us.
10   O God, how long will the enemy mock you?
      Will the enemy revile your Name forever?
11   Why hold back your hand, your right hand?
      Take it from the folds of your cloak and destroy them!

12   O God, my Sovereign of old,
      you bring deliverance throughout all the earth—
13   you stirred up the sea by your might;
      you smashed the heads of dragons in the waters,
14   you crushed the heads of Leviathan,
      and offered it to the desert tribes for food.

15 You released the springs and torrents;
    you brought dry land out of the primeval waters.
16 Yours is the day, and yours the night;
    you established the moon and the sun.
17 You fixed all the limits of the land;
    summer and winter you made.

18 Now remember how the enemy has blasphemed you, Adonai,
    and how a stupid people has reviled your Name!
19 Don't give the vulture the life of your dove;
    don't ignore forever the lives of your little ones!
20 Look to your Covenant,
    because the dark places in the land
    are filled with haunts of violence!
21 Don't let the downtrodden turn away in disappointment—
    let the oppressed and poor praise your Name!
22 Arise, O God, and champion your cause;
    remember how the fool mocks you day after day!
23 Don't ignore the shouts of your enemies—
    the uproar of those who rebel against you
    is getting louder and louder.

75

To the conductor: to the tune of "Do Not Destroy"
A psalm of Asaph
A song

1   Thank you, O God, thank you!
    For your presence—your Name—is near
    when we hear of your wonderful deeds.

2   "I choose the right time—
    I who judge with absolute justice.
3   When the earth quakes and shakes all who live on it,
    I'm the one who makes its pillars firm."

4   To the arrogant I say,
    "Forsake your pride!"
    and to the corrupt,
    "Do not raise your proud horns!
5   Don't raise your horns against the Exalted One
    or speak arrogantly against the Rock of Ages."

6   No power from the east or west
    or even from the wilderness
    can raise a person up—
7   God alone is judge;
    God brings one down and raises up another.
8   In the hand of Our God there is a cup,
    and the wine foams in it, hot with spice;
    Our God pours it out,
    and all the wicked of the earth drink it
    and drain it to its very dregs.

9   As for me, I will declare all this forever;
    I will sing praises to the God of our ancestors.
10 "I will break off the horns of the wicked,
    but the horns of the righteous will be lifted high."

76

To the conductor: for strings
By Asaph
A song

1   O God, you made yourself known in Judah;
    your Name is great in Israel—
2   you set up your tent in Salem,
    and Zion is your home.
3   There you broke the fiery arrows,
    the shield, the sword, the weapons of war.
          —— *Selah* ——
4   You are resplendent with light,
    majestic on the mountains of the Lion:
5   their bravest warriors, despoiled, slept in death;
    not a single warrior was able to lift a hand.
6   At your blast, O God of our ancestors,
    both horse and chariots lie still.
7   You and you alone are to be worshiped.
    Who can stand when your anger is roused?
8   You pronounced your sentence from the heavens;
    the earth in terror was silent
9   when you arose to execute judgment,
    to save the lowly of the earth.
10 Indeed, they will praise you
    for the wrath you pour out on others,
and those who escape your wrath
    will gather around you.

11 So make vows to Adonai, your God—
    and fulfill them.
Let neighboring lands bring their tribute
    to the One who strikes terror,
12 who cuts short the breath of their leaders,
    and strikes terror in the rulers of the earth.

77

To the conductor: for Jeduthun
By Asaph
A psalm

¹ I cried to God for help,
   I cried out to God to hear me.
² In the day of my distress I sought you, Adonai,
   and by night I lifted my outstretched hand in prayer.
   I lay sweating and nothing would cool me,
   nothing could comfort me.
³ When I called you to mind, I groaned;
   as I lay thinking, gloom overcame my spirit.
                —— *Selah* ——
⁴ You kept my eyes open all night;
   I was so troubled I couldn't speak.
⁵ My thoughts went back to times now distant,
   to years long past;
⁶ I remembered my songs in the night.
   As I lay thinking,
   my spirit pondered:
⁷ "Adonai, will you reject us forever and ever?
   Will you never again show your favor?
⁸ Has your unfailing love now vanished forever?
   Will your promise remain unfulfilled
   generation after generation?
⁹ Have you forgotten how to show mercy, O God?
   Has your anger blotted out your compassion?"
                —— *Selah* ——

¹⁰ Then I thought: "This is the cause of my infirmity—
    it is another visitation of the right hand of the Most High!"
¹¹ And then I remember your deeds, Adonai—
    yes, I will call to mind your wonderful acts of long ago.
¹² I will meditate on all your works,
    and think about all you have done.
¹³ O God, your way is holy;
    what god is as great as Our God?
¹⁴ You are the God who worked miracles;
    you have shown the nations your power.

15 With your strong arm you redeemed your people,
    the descendants of Israel and their children's children.
16 The waters saw you, O God,
    they saw you and trembled,
    and the ocean depths quaked.
17 The clouds coursed their waters,
    the skies echoed with your voice,
    your arrows flashed all around.
18 The sound of your thunder was in the whirlwind,
    your lightning lit up the world,
    and the earth shook and quaked.
19 You made your path through the sea,
    and walked through the mighty waters,
    yet no one could find your footsteps.
20 You guided your people like a flock of sheep,
    by the hand of Moses and Miriam and Aaron.

78

An instructional psalm
By Asaph

1 My people, hear my teaching;
  listen to the words of my mouth!
2 I will open my mouth in parables,
  I will utter things hidden from of old—
3 the things we have heard and known,
  things our ancestors have told us.
4 We won't hide them from our children,
  we will tell the next generation.

We'll tell them of your praiseworthy deeds, Adonai,
  your power, and the wonders you have performed.
5 You set up statutes for our forebears,
  and established the Law in Israel,
  which you commanded our ancestors to teach their children
6 so the next generation would know them—
  children yet to be born—
and as they come up,
  they would tell their own children.
7 Then they would put their trust in you
  and not forget your deeds, but keep your commandments—
8 unlike their ancestors,
  a stubborn and defiant generation,
whose hearts were fickle,
  whose spirits were unfaithful to God.

9 Like the Ephraimite archers
  who turned tail in the day of battle,
10 they didn't keep your Covenant,
  and refused to live by your Law.
11 They forgot your deeds,
  the wonders you showed them.
12 In the sight of their ancestors, you performed miracles
  in the land of Egypt, on the plain of Zoan.

¹³ You split the sea and led them through it;
    you made the water stand like a wall.
¹⁴ You guided them with a cloud by day,
    and by night with the light of a fire.
¹⁵ You split the rock in the wilderness
    and gave them water that gushed like the great seas—
¹⁶ you brought streams out of the rocky crag,
    and made water flow down like rivers.

¹⁷ But still they sinned against you,
    defying the Most High in the wilderness.
¹⁸ They willfully challenged God
    by demanding food for themselves.
¹⁹ They spoke against you:
    they said, "Can God prepare a feast in the wilderness?
²⁰ True, Moses struck the rock and water gushed out,
    and streams flowed abundantly.
    But can God also give us bread
    and provide meat for the people?"
²¹ When you heard them, Adonai, you were enraged;
    your fire blazed up against the people,
    and your wrath erupted against Israel
²² because they didn't believe in you
    or trust that you would deliver them.

²³ Yet you gave a command to the skies above
    and opened the doors of the heavens;
²⁴ you rained down manna for them to eat,
    and gave them grain from heaven.
²⁵ Mere mortals ate the bread of angels;
    you sent them food in abundance.
²⁶ You loosed the east wind in the heavens
    and drove the south wind by your power.
²⁷ You rained meat down on them like dust,
    winged fowl like sand on the seashore.
²⁸ You made birds come down into their camp
    and around their tents.
²⁹ They ate until they were fully satisfied;
    you gave them what they craved.

30 And still they did not desist from complaining—
   even while it was still in their mouths.
31 So you rose in anger against them,
   killing the strongest among them,
   and striking down the youth of Israel.
32 Even so, they kept on sinning;
   in spite of your wonders, they didn't believe,
33 so you made their days vanish like a vapor,
   and their years pass by like a phantom in the night.

34 Whenever you struck them down, they would turn to you;
   they became eager for you again.
35 They remembered that God was their rock,
   that God Most High was their redeemer.
36 But then they would deceive you with their speech,
   and lie to you with their lips;
37 their hearts were fickle,
   they were unfaithful to your Covenant.

38 But you were merciful;
   you forgave their wrongs
   and didn't destroy them.
   Time and again, you held back your anger
   and didn't give vent to your full wrath.
39 You remembered that they were but flesh,
   a passing breath that never returns.

40 How often they rebelled against you in the wilderness,
   and grieved you in the wasteland!
41 Again and again they challenged you;
   they pushed the Holy One of Israel to the limit.
42 They didn't remember your power
   or the day you ransomed them from the oppressor,
43 the day you displayed your miraculous signs in Egypt,
   or your wonders in the plain of Zoan.

44 You turned their rivers to blood,
   and made their streams undrinkable.
45 You sent swarms of flies to devour them
   and frogs to devastate them.
46 You gave their crops to grasshoppers,
   and their produce to locusts.

47 You killed their vines with hail
    and their sycamores with sleet.
48 You abandoned their cattle to the hail,
    and their livestock to lightning bolts.
49 You unleashed your blazing anger against them—
    your fury, rage and havoc—
with an escort of avenging angels
50   who cleared a path for your anger.
You didn't spare them from death,
    but gave them over to pestilence.
51 You struck down all Egypt's firstborn,
    the firstfruits of their vigor in the tents of Ham.
52 But you led your people like a flock,
    and guided them like sheep through the wilderness.
53 You led them to safety, so they were not afraid,
    while the seas covered their enemies.
54 You brought them to the foot of your holy hill,
    to the mountain your right hand had won.
55 You drove out nations before them;
    you allotted their lands to them as an inheritance.
You settled the tribes of Israel in their tents.

56 But again they challenged and defied you;
    they did not keep your statutes.
57 Like their ancestors they were fickle and cynical,
    they recoiled like a faulty bow.
58 They angered you with their hillside altars,
    and aroused your jealousy with their idols.
59 When you heard them, you were enraged,
    and utterly rejected Israel.
60 You abandoned the tabernacle at Shiloh,
    the tent you had pitched in their midst.
61 You let the ark of your might go into captivity,
    your glory into the hands of the enemy.
62 You gave over your people to the sword,
    you were furious with the people of your inheritance.
63 Fire consumed their young men,
    and their young women sang no wedding songs;
64 their priests fell by the sword,
    and their widows had no tears left to cry.

65 Then you awoke as from sleep,
    as a warrior wakes from the stupor of wine.
66 You beat back their enemies
    and put them to everlasting shame.
67 Then you rejected the clan of Joseph,
    you did not choose the tribe of Ephraim;
68 instead, you chose the tribe of Judah,
    Mount Zion, which you loved.
69 You built your sanctuary like the high heavens,
    like the earth that you established forever;
70 you chose David, your faithful one
    and took him from the sheepfolds;
71 you took him from tending nursing ewes
    to be the shepherd of your chosen people, Israel.
72 And David tended them with blameless heart;
    leading them with skillful hands.

79

A psalm of Asaph

1 O God, the nations have invaded your domain,
    they have defiled your holy Temple!
    They have reduced Jerusalem to a pile of ruins!
2 They have left the corpses of your faithful ones
        to the birds of the air,
    and the flesh of your devout to the beasts of the earth.
3 They have shed blood like water throughout Jerusalem,
    with no one left to bury the dead!
4 And now we're insulted by our neighbors,
    the laughingstock of those around us, the butt of their jokes.

5 How much longer will you be angry with us, Adonai?
    Forever?
    Will your jealousy go on smoldering like a fire?
6 Redirect your anger to the nations,
        who do not acknowledge you,
    and to those dominions
        that do not call on your Name,
7 for they have devoured your people
    and reduced their home to desolation.
8 Don't hold our former sins against us.
    In your tenderness, quickly intervene,
    for we can hardly be crushed lower.
9 Help us, O God of our salvation,
    for the sake of your glorious Name!
    Deliver us! Atone for our sins
        and rescue us for your Name's sake!
10 Why should the nations ask, "Where is their God?"
    Soon, let us see the nations learn what vengeance you exact
    for the blood of your faithful shed there.
11 May the groans of the captives reach you;
    with your long arm, rescue those condemned to death.
12 Pay back our neighbors sevenfold, and strike them to the heart
    for the monstrous insults they hurled at you, Adonai.
13 Then we, your people, the flock of your pasture
        will give you everlasting thanks;
    we will recount your praises
        forever and ever.

To the conductor: to the tune of "Lilies of the Covenant"
By Asaph
A psalm

1 Shepherd of Israel, hear us,
     you who lead Joseph like a flock!
You who are enthroned on the cherubim, shine out!
2   Shine out before Ephraim, Benjamin and Manasseh!
Awaken your power
     and come to save us!

3 *O God, return to us—*
     let your face smile on us, and we will be saved!

4 Adonai, God of Hosts,
     how much longer will you fume
     while your people pray?
5 You fed us on the bread of tears,
     and made us drink our tears in such measure;
6 you now let our neighbors ridicule us
     and our enemies treat us with scorn.

7 *O God of Hosts, return to us—*
     let your face smile on us and we will be saved!

8 There was a vine:
     you uprooted it from Egypt;
     to plant it, you drove out other nations.
9 You cleared a space where it could grow;
     it took root and filled the land—
10 it covered the mountains with its shade,
     and its branches were like the cedars of God;
11 its tendrils stretched out to the Sea,
     its offshoots all the way to the Euphrates.
12 Why, then, have you destroyed its wall
     so that all who pass can steal its grapes?
13 The forest boar can trample it
     and creatures of the field can eat it.

14 Please, O God of Hosts, come back!
    Look down from heaven,
    and watch over this vine,
15 the root planted by your own hand,
    the shoot you have raised up as your own.
16 It is now cut down and thrown into the fire,
    consumed by the flames of your rebuke.
17 Let your hand rest upon the One at your right side,
    the Chosen One you raised up for yourself.
18 Then we'll never turn from you again;
    our life renewed, we will invoke your Name.

19 *Adonai, God of Hosts, return to us—*
    let your face smile on us and we will be saved!

81

To the conductor: for the Gittite harp
By Asaph

1 Sing out in praise of God our strength,
    acclaim the God of our ancestors!
2 Begin the music, take up the tambourine,
    the tuneful harp and the lyre!
3 Blow the trumpet on the New Moon,
    and on the Full Moon, the day of our Feast.
4 For this is a law for Israel,
    a decree of the God of our forebears,
5 laid as a solemn charge on Joseph
    when he went from the land of Egypt.

Then I heard language
    too great to comprehend:
6 "When I lifted the burden from your shoulders,
    your hands were freed from the builder's basket.
7 When you cried to me in distress,
    I rescued you.

I answered you cloaked in thunder;
    and even though you challenged me
    by the waters of Meribah.
—— Selah ——

8 Listen, my people, while I accuse you—
    if only you would listen to me, Israel!
9 You will have no alien god among you
    nor bow down to any foreign god.
10 I am Adonai, your God,
    who brought you out of the land of Egypt!
11 But my people did not listen to my voice
    and Israel would not obey me;
12 so I gave them over to their willful hearts,
    to follow their own devices.
13 If only my people would listen to me,
    if Israel would follow my paths,
14 I would subdue their enemies at once
    and turn my hand against their persecutors.
15 Those who hate me will come cringing before me,
    and meet with everlasting punishment.
16 And I will feed Israel with the finest wheat
    and satisfy you with honey from the rock."

A psalm by Asaph

1   God presides in the divine assembly
     and pronounces judgment among the "gods":

2   "How long will you defend the unjust
     and show partiality to the corrupt?
3   Defend the lowly and the orphaned,
     render justice to the oppressed and the destitute!
4   Rescue the weak and the poor,
     and save them from the hand of violence!
5   But you know nothing and you understand nothing—
     you walk in darkness,
  and the foundations of the earth
     are shaking because of your ignorance!
6   I said, 'You are "gods," all of you—
     children of the Most High!'
7   But you will die as any mortal,
     and fall like any ruler!"

8   Rise up, O God, and bring justice to the earth,
     for all the nations are your possession!

1 O God, don't be silent;
        don't be aloof, don't be quiet, O God!
2 Look what an uproar your enemies are making!
        Your foes have reared their ugly heads.
3 They cunningly plot against your people
        and conspire against those you cherish.
4 They say, "Come, let's destroy them as a nation;
        let the name of Israel be remembered no more!"
5 Indeed, they lay their plans with a single purpose
        and form an alliance against you—
6 the tents of Edom and the Ishmaelites,
        Moab and the descendants of Hagar,
7 Byblos, Ammon and Amalek,
        Philistia with the inhabitants of Tyre—
8 even Assyria has joined them,
        lending support to the children of Lot.
9 Treat them as you did Midian,
        as you treated Sisera and Jabin at the river Kishon,
10 who were destroyed at Endor
        and became dung for the field.
11 Treat their nobles like Oreb and Zeeb,
        and their people like Zebah and Zalmunna,
12 who said, "Let's take possession
        of the pastures of God."
13 My God, make them like whirling dust,
        like chaff blown by the wind!
14 As fire consumes a forest
        and flame sets the hills ablaze,
15 pursue them with your storm
        and terrify them with your whirlwind!
16 Fill their faces with shame,
        and make them seek your Name, Adonai!
17 Let them always be frustrated and terrified,
        and let them perish in disgrace.
18 Make them know that your Name alone—Adonai—
        is supreme over all the earth.

84

To the conductor: for the Gittite harp
By the disciples of Qorach

1 How I love your dwelling place,
   Adonai Sabaoth!
2 How my soul yearns and pines
   for your courts, Adonai!
   My heart and my flesh sing for joy
   to you, the living God.
3 The sparrow has found its home at last,
   the swallow a nest for its young—
   on your altars, Adonai Sabaoth,
   my Sovereign, my God!
4 Happiness belongs to those who live in your house
   and can praise you all day long;
                —— *Selah* ——
5 and happy the pilgrims who find refuge in you
   as they set their hearts on the Ascents!
6 As they go through the Valley of the Weeper,
   they make it a place of springs,
   clothed in blessings by the early rains.
7 From there they make their way from village to village,
   until each one appears before God in Zion.

8 Adonai, God of Hosts, hear my prayer;
   Listen, O God of our ancestors!
                —— *Selah* ——
9 O God, our shield, show us your favor
   and look upon the face of your Anointed—
10 for a single day in your courts
   is worth more than a thousand anywhere else;
   better to be a humble doorkeeper in God's house
   than to live richly in the tents of the corrupt.
11 For you, Adonai our God, are a battlement and shield,
   bestowing grace and glory;
   Our God withholds nothing good
   from those whose walk is blameless.
12 Adonai Sabaoth,
   happy are those who put their trust in you!

85

For the conductor
By the disciples of Qorach
A psalm

1   Adonai, favor your land once again
     and restore the fortunes of Israel;
2   forgive the guilt of your people
     and cover all their sins.
3   Set aside all your anger,
     and calm the heat of your rage.
4   Return to us, O God of our deliverance!
     Put an end to your displeasure with us.
5   Will you be angry with us forever,
     will your wrath continue from one generation to the next?
6   Won't you revive us again
     so that your people can rejoice in you?
7   Let us see your mercy, Adonai,
     and grant us your deliverance.

8   I will listen to what you have to say, Adonai—
     a voice that speaks of peace,
  peace for your people and your friends
     so long as they don't return to their folly.
9   Your salvation is near for those who revere you
     and your glory will dwell in our land.
10   Love and faithfulness have met;
     justice and peace have embraced.
11   Fidelity will sprout from the earth
     and justice will lean down from heaven.
12   Our God will give us what is good,
     and our land will yield its harvest.
13   Justice will march before you, Adonai,
     and peace will prepare the way for your steps.

A prayer of David

1   Open your ears, Adonai, and answer me,
     for I am weak and helpless.
2   Save me from death,
     for I am loyal to you;
  protect your faithful one,
     for you are my God and I trust in you.
3   Have mercy on me, Adonai,
     for I pray to you all day long.
4   Make your faithful one glad,
     for I lift my soul to you, Adonai.

5   You are good and forgiving, Adonai,
     full of constant love for all who call on you.
6   Listen to my prayer, Adonai,
     hear my cries for help.
7   I call to you in times of trouble
     because you answer my prayer.
8   There is no other god like you, Adonai,
     not one who can do what you do.
9   When you act, all the nations will come
     and bow down before you, Adonai,
     and will pay honor to your Name.
10   How great you are, Worker of Marvels;
     you alone are God!
11   Teach me your way, Adonai,
     so that I may walk with you alone;
     make me single-hearted in reverence for your Name.
12   I will praise you with all my heart, Adonai;
     I will glorify your Name forever.
13   How great is your constant love for me!
     You have rescued me from the depths of Sheol.

14   O God, the arrogant are coming against me;
     a ruthless gang is trying to kill me—
     they don't care that you are my Leader.
15   But you, Adonai, are a compassionate and merciful God,
     slow to anger, overflowing with love and fidelity.

16 Turn to me and have mercy on me;
   grant me strength, for I am faithful to you
   just as my parents were.
17 Give me a sign of your favor,
   then those who hate me will be frustrated
when they see that you, Adonai,
   have given me comfort and help.

87

By the disciples of Qorach
A psalm
A song

1 Our God loves this city
   founded on the holy mountain;
2 God loves the gates of Zion
   more than all the dwellings of Israel,
3 and glorious predictions are made about you,
   the city of God:
                —— *Selah* ——
4 "I will add monstrous Egypt, and Babylon
   to the nations that acknowledge me.
Philistia, Tyre, Ethiopia—
   each of them was born there."
5 Indeed, it will be said that everyone
   was born in Zion,
and the Most High will be the one
   who brings it all to pass.
6 Our God will write in the register of the peoples,
   "This one too was born there."
7 People in Zion will dance as they sing,
   "Everything I am has its source in you."

88

A song
A psalm by the disciples of Qorach
To the conductor: to the tune of "Sickness and Depression"
A teaching psalm by Heman the Ezraite

1 Adonai, God of my deliverance,
   by day I cry out to you,
   in the night I am before you.
2 Let my prayer reach you;
   turn your ear to my cry!
3 Troubles fill me to the brim,
   and my life is on the brink of Sheol;
4 I am numbered among those who go down into the Pit,
   all my strength is drained from me.
5 I am alone, down among the dead,
   like a body lying in its grave—
   I'm like someone you no longer remember,
   someone cut off from your care.
6 You have plunged me into the lowest part of the Pit,
   into its deepest and darkest regions,
7 with the weight of your anger pulling me down,
   drowning me beneath the waves of your fury.
          —— *Selah* ——
8 You have turned my friends against me
   and made me repulsive to them;
   I am in prison and there is no escape,
9   and my eyes ache from crying.

   Adonai, I call you all day long,
   I stretch out my hands to you.
10 Are your wonders meant for the dead?
   Can ghosts rise up to praise you?
11 Who declares your love in the grave,
   or your fidelity from the place of destruction?
12 Do they hear about your marvels in the netherworld,
   about your justice in the Land of the Forgotten?
13 But I am here, calling for your help,
   praying to Adonai every morning.

14 Why do you reject me, Adonai?
    Why do you hide your face from me?
15 I am close to death and in despair—
    I've suffered your terrors since I was a child.
16 You consumed me with your anger
    and destroyed me with your terrors;
17 they surrounded me like a flood all day long,
    and engulfed me altogether.
18 You've turned my friends and loved ones against me;
    now night is my closest companion.

89

A teaching psalm by Ethan the Ezraite

1 Forever I will sing the wonders of your love, Adonai,
    proclaiming your faithfulness to all generations!
2 I'll tell them that your love stands firm forever,
    your fidelity is fixed in the heavens.
3 "I have made a covenant with my chosen;
    sworn an oath to David, my faithful one:
4 'I will establish your line forever,
    and make your throne firm throughout all generations.' "

5 The heavens praise your wonders, Adonai,
    and the council of the holy ones declares your fidelity.
6 Who in the skies can be compared to Our God?
    Who is like Adonai among the gods—
7 a God who is revered in the council of the holy ones
    great and awesome above all others?
8 Adonai Sabaoth, who is like you?
    Power and faithfulness surround you!
9 You rule the surging sea,
    calming the turmoil of its waves.
10 You crush the monster Rahab with a mortal blow,
    and scatter your enemies with your strong arm.
11 The heavens are yours, and so is the earth—
    you established the world and all it contains.

12 You created North and South;
    Mounts Tabor and Hermon echo your Name.
13 Your arm is powerful, your hand is strong,
    your right hand is lifted high.
14 Your judgment seat is built on righteousness and justice,
    love and fidelity stand in your presence.

15 Happy are those who have learned to praise you, Adonai,
    who walk in the light of your presence!
16 They will rejoice in your Name all day long,
    uplifted by your justice.
17 You are the strength in which they glory;
    through your favor we hold our heads high.
18 Our God is our shield;
    the holy One of Israel is our ruler.

19 One day a vision came
    and you announced this to your faithful ones:
    "I have bestowed power on a warrior
    and raised up a youth from among the people.
20 I have discovered David,
    who is faithful to me.
    David, I anoint you with my holy oil.
21   My hand will be ready to help you,
    and my arm to give you strength.
22 No enemy will oppress you
    and no rebel will bring you low;
23 I will shatter your foes before you,
    and strike down those who hate you.
24 My fidelity and love will be with you,
    and through my Name your strength will increase.
25 I will extend your rule to the Sea
    and your dominion as far as the Euphrates.
26 You will say to me,
    'You are my Abba, my God,
    my rock and my deliverance.'
27 And I will appoint you my firstborn,
    higher than all the earth's rulers.
28 I will maintain my love for you forever
    and my covenant with you will never fail.
29 I will establish your line forever
    and your throne as long as the heavens endure.

30 If your descendants forsake my Law
and do not live by my rules,
31 if they renounce my teachings
and do not observe my commands,
32 I will punish their disobedience with the rod
and their iniquity with lashes.
33 But I will never deprive them of my steadfast love—
I'll never betray my faithfulness.
34 I will not violate my Covenant
or change what my lips have promised.
35 I have sworn by my holiness once and for all,
I will not break my word.
36 Your line will continue forever,
your throne will stand before me like the sun.
37 It will be established forever,
as faithful as the moon's witness in the skies."
—— *Selah* ——

38 Yet you have rejected and spurned
and raged against your Anointed!
39 You have repudiated the Covenant with your faithful ones,
defiled the crown and flung it to the ground.
40 You have breached my walls
and left my fortresses in ruin;
41 all who pass by plunder me
and I have become the laughingstock of my neighbors.
42 You have increased the power of my enemies
and made my adversaries rejoice;
43 you have blunted my sword
and refused to help me in battle.
44 You have put an end to a glorious reign
and hurled my throne to the ground.
45 You have cut short the days of my youth
and covered me with shame.
—— *Selah* ——

46 How long, Adonai, will you hide yourself from sight?
Will your wrath blaze like fire forever?
47 Remember how fleeting life is—
have you created humankind in vain?

48 Who can live and not see death
   or save themselves from the power of Sheol?
49 Where is your steadfast love of old, Adonai,
   those faithful promises you swore to David?
50 Remember the abuse hurled at your faithful one, Adonai,
   how I have borne in my heart the taunts of entire nations;
51 how your enemies have vilified us, Adonai,
   vilified your Anointed at every step!

52 Blessed be Our God forever!
   Amen, amen!

book IV

90

A prayer of Moses, chosen one of God

1 Adonai, you have been our refuge
    from one generation to the next.
2 Before the mountains were born,
    you brought forth the earth and the world,
    you are God without beginning or end.
3 You turn humankind back into dust
    and say: "Go back, creatures of the earth!"
4 For in your sight a thousand years
    are like yesterday, come and gone,
    no more than a watch in the night.
5 You sweep us away like a dream,
    fleeting as the grass that springs up in the morning—
6 in the morning it sprouts,
    but by evening it has withered and died.

7 In the same way, we are consumed—
    terrified by your anger and indignation.
8 Our guilt lies open before you;
    our secrets are revealed in the light of your presence.
9 All our days pass away under your anger,
    and our life is over like a sigh.
10 The span of our life is but seventy years—
    perhaps eighty if we're strong—
  but the best of them are nothing but sorrow and pain;
    they pass swiftly and we are gone.
11 Who understands the power of your anger?
    We fear the strength of your wrath.

12   Make us realize how short life is
        that we may gain wisdom of heart.

13   Adonai, relent!
        How long before you have mercy on your faithful ones?
14   When morning comes, fill us with your love,
        and we will celebrate all our days.
15   Give us joy for as many days as you afflicted us,
        for as many years as we knew misfortune!
16   Let your work be seen by your faithful,
        your glory be witnessed by their children.
17   Let our God's favor be upon us!
        Grant success to the work of our hands,
        success to the work of our hands!

91

1   You who dwell in the shelter of the Most High
        and pass the night in the shadow of Shaddai,
2   say: "Adonai, my refuge and my mountain fortress,
        my God in whom I trust!"
3   For Our God says:
        "I will rescue you from the snare,
        and shield you from poisoned arrows.
4   I will cover you with my pinions;
        under my wings you will take refuge;
        my faithfulness will shield you.
5   You have no need to fear the prowlers of the night
        or the arrow that flies by day,
6   the plague that lurks in the shadows
        or the scourge that stalks at noon.
7   Though a thousand fall at your left side
        and ten thousand at your right,
        it will never come near you.
8   You will see it pass you by,
        and witness the punishment of the corrupt
        with your own eyes.

9   Because you have made me your refuge
        and have me as your stronghold,
10 no evil will befall you,
        and no disaster will come near your tent.
11 For I will command my angels
        to guard you wherever you go.
12 They'll carry you in their hands
        so you don't hurt your foot on a stone.
13 You'll tread on the young lion as easily as one does a cobra;
        you'll trample down both lion and serpent.
14 Because you love me, I will deliver you;
        I will rescue you because you acknowledge my Name.
15 You will call upon me, and I will answer you;
        I will be with you in trouble;
        I will deliver you and honor you.
16 I will satisfy you with a long life
        and show you my salvation."

A psalm
A song for the Sabbath

¹   It is good to praise you, Adonai,
     and celebrate your Name in song, Most High—
²   to proclaim your love in the morning
     and your fidelity through the watches of the night,
³   to the music of a ten-stringed lyre
     and the melody of the harp.
⁴   Your deeds, Adonai, fill me with joy;
     I shout in triumph over the work of your hands.
⁵   How great are your works, Adonai!
     How profound your thoughts!

⁶   Those who don't realize this are senseless;
     they are fools because they can't understand
⁷   that though the corrupt keep springing up like grass
     and all evildoers blossom and flourish,
     it is only so that they will be destroyed forever—
⁸   while you, Adonai, reign on high forever!
⁹   Come and watch your foes, Adonai,
     come and watch your foes perish
     and all evildoers will be scattered.
¹⁰   I have raised my horn high,
     strong as the wild ox;
     I am anointed with fine oil.
¹¹   With my own eyes I've seen the defeat of my enemies,
     and I've heard the downfall of my cruel foes.

¹²   The just flourish like a palm tree,
     and grow as tall as the cedars of Lebanon;
¹³   transplanted in the house of Our God,
     they flourish in the courts of the Most High—
¹⁴   still full of sap in old age,
     they still produce abundant fruit,
¹⁵   eager to declare that Our God is just—
     my rock, in whom there is no wrong.

1 Our God reigns, robed in splendor!
  You are robed, Adonai, and armed with strength.
  The world stands firm and cannot be moved;
2   your throne stands firm from ages past,
    from eternity you exist.
3 The seas are shouting, Adonai—
    the seas raise their voices,
    the seas shout with pounding waves.
4 Stronger than the thunder of the great waters,
    mightier than the breakers of the sea,
    mightiest of all is Our God!
5 Your reign was made known from of old;
    the holy ones praise you in your Temple,
    Adonai, for days without end.

1 Adonai, God our avenger—
    reveal yourself, God our avenger!
2 Rise up, judge of the earth,
    and give the arrogant what they deserve!
3 How long will these violent gangs, Adonai,
    how long will these violent gangs be jubilant?
4 Arrogance pours forth from their speech
    as they boast about all their crimes.
5 They crush your people, Adonai!
    They oppress those most dear to you!
6 They prey on the elderly and attack foreigners,
    and murder children who beg in the streets.
7 They say, "God doesn't see us;
    the God of Israel doesn't notice!"

8   Wise up, you fools!
        You idiots! When will you ever learn?
9   Can't the One who fashioned the ear, hear?
        Can't the Maker of the eye, see?
10 Do you think that the One who disciplines entire nations
        won't punish a guilty individual?
    Do you think the Teacher of humankind
        doesn't already know?
11 Our God knows what people think—
        and knows just how vapid their reasoning is!

12 Those you instruct are the fortunate ones, Adonai,
        because you teach them from your Law—
13 to give them tranquility in times of trouble,
        until a pitfall is dug for the treacherous.
14 Our God will not abandon the faithful
        and will not desert those who belong to the Covenant.
15 The Tribunal of Justice will restore equity,
        and all who are upright in heart will follow it.

16 I said, "Who will take my side against the corrupt?
        Who will stand by me against the violent?"
17 If Our God had not helped me,
        I would have gone quickly to the land of silence.
18 I said, "I am falling,"
        but your constant love, Adonai, upheld me.
19 When I am anxious and worried,
        you comfort me and bring me joy.
20 You have nothing to do with those
        who sit on the thrones of iniquity,
    nor do those who cause strife
        receive your protection.
21 They plotted against the life of the just,
        and sentenced the innocent to death from their hiding places.
22 But Adonai is my fortress;
        my God is my rock of refuge.
23 God will make their evil recoil upon them,
        and destroy them through their corruption;
        Adonai, Our God, will utterly destroy them.

1 Come, let us sing joyfully to God!
    Raise a shout to our rock, our deliverance!
2 Let us come into God's presence with thanksgiving,
    and sing our praises with joy.
3 For Our God is a great God,
    the great Ruler, above all gods.
4 O God, in your hands are the depths of the earth,
    and the mountain peaks are yours.
5 Yours is the sea, for you made it,
    the dry land as well, for your hands formed it.
6 Come, let us bow down in worship;
    let us kneel before Adonai, our Maker.
7 For you are our God,
    and we are the people you shepherd,
    the flock under your care.

If only you would hear God's voice today!
8 "Harden not your hearts as at Meribah,
    as in the days of Massah in the desert,
9 where your ancestors tested me;
    they tested me even though they had seen my works.
10 For forty years that generation provoked me,
    until I said, 'The hearts of these people go astray,
    and they do not know my ways.'
11 Then I took an oath in anger,
    'They will never come to my place of rest.' "

1 Sing to Our God a new song!
    Sing to Our God, all the earth!
2 Sing to Our God, bless God's Name!
    Proclaim God's salvation day after day;
3 declare God's glory among the nations,
    God's marvels to every people.
4 Our God is great, most worthy of praise,
    Our God is to be revered above all gods.
5 The gods of the nations are nothing, they don't exist—
    but Our God created the universe.
6 In God's presence are splendor and majesty,
    in God's sanctuary power and beauty.
7 Pay tribute to Our God, you tribes of the people,
    pay tribute to the God of glory and power.
8 Pay tribute to the glorious Name of Our God;
    bring out the offering, and carry it into God's courts.
9 Worship Our God, majestic in holiness,
    tremble in God's presence, all the earth!
10 Say among the nations,
    "Our God reigns supreme!"
The world stands firm and unshakable:
    Our God will judge each nation with strict justice.
11 Let the heavens be glad, let the earth rejoice,
    let the sea roar and all that it holds!
12 Let the fields exult and all that is in them!
    Let all the trees of the forest sing for joy
13 at the presence of Our God, for God is coming,
    God is coming to rule the earth—
to rule the world with justice
    and its peoples with truth!

1   Our God reigns!
      Let the earth rejoice;
      let the many coastlands be glad!

2   Clouds and thick darkness surround you, Adonai;
      righteousness and justice
      are the foundation of your judgment seat.
3   Fire goes before you
      and destroys your enemies on every side.
4   Your lightning bolts light up the world;
      the earth sees, and trembles.
5   The mountains melt like wax at your sight,
      at the sight of the God of all the earth.

6   The heavens proclaim your justice,
      and all the peoples see your glory.
7   All who worship images are put to shame,
      who make their boast in worthless idols,
      all gods bow down before you.
8   Zion hears and is glad,
      and the women of Judah rejoice
      because of your judgments, Adonai.
9   For you, Adonai, are Most High over all the earth;
      you are exalted far above all gods.

10   Adonai, you love those who hate evil;
      preserve the lives of your faithful ones
      and deliver them from the hands of the wicked.
11   Light dawns for the just,
      and joy for the upright in heart.
12   Rejoice in Our God, you just,
      and give praise to God's holy Name!

98

A psalm

1 Sing a new song to Our God,
    who has worked wonders,
whose right hand and holy arm
    have brought deliverance!
2 Our God has made salvation known
    and shown divine justice to the nations,
3 and has remembered in truth and love
    the house of Israel.
All the ends of the earth have seen
    the salvation of our God.
4 Shout to the Most High, all the earth,
    break into joyous songs of praise!
5 Sing praise to Our God with the harp,
    with the harp and melodious singing!
6 With trumpets and the blast of the shofar,
    raise a shout to Our God, Ruler of All.
7 Let the sea and all within it thunder;
    the world and all its peoples.
8 Let the rivers clap their hands
    and the hills ring out their joy
9 before Our God, who comes to judge the earth,
    who will rule the world with justice
    and its peoples with equity.

1 Our God reigns,
   and the nations tremble!
You who are enthroned on the cherubim,
   let the earth quake!
2 Our God is even higher than Zion,
   and exalted above all the nations;
3 let them praise your Name,
   Great and Awesome One:

"You are holy 4 and mighty,
   a Leader who loves justice,
who established honesty, justice and righteousness in Israel!
   You have done this!
5 We exalt you, Adonai, Our God,
   and we worship at your footstool.
   You are holy!"

6 Miriam, Moses and Aaron were among them,
   and Samuel too was among those who invoked the Name;
they called on Our God
   and God answered them.
7 Adonai spoke to them in the pillar of cloud;
   they obeyed the decrees and statutes God gave them.
8 Adonai, Our God, you answered them.
   For them, you became God the Forgiver
   even though you punished their evil deeds.

9 "We exalt you, Adonai our God,
   and we worship at your holy mountain;
   for you, Adonai our God, are holy!"

A psalm for the thanksgiving offering

1 Acclaim Our God with joy,
   all the earth!
2 Serve Our God with gladness!
   Enter into God's presence with a joyful song!
3 Know that Adonai is God!
   Our God made us, and we belong to the Creator;
we are God's people
   and the sheep of God's pasture.
4 Enter God's gates with thanksgiving
   and the courts with praise!
Give thanks to God!
   Bless God's Name!
5 For Our God is good;
   God's steadfast love endures forever,
and God's faithfulness
   to all generations.

1 I sing of your love and justice—
   Adonai, I sing to you!
2 I will be faithful in my pursuit of you;
   when will you come to me?
   I will strive to live in purity of heart among my peers;
3 I will not look upon any injustice without acting.
   I hate crooked dealing, and will have none of it.
4 Twisted thoughts are far from me—
   I will have nothing to do with evil.
5 Those backbiters who slander their neighbor—
   I will silence them;
   those with haughty looks and proud hearts—
   I will not tolerate them.
6 I look to those who keep faith with the land
   to make up my household;
   only those who follow a blameless path
   will I allow in my company.
7 There is no room in my house for any deceiver;
   no liars will stand in my presence.
8 Morning after morning I will silence
   all who are corrupt in the land,
   and cut off all evildoers
   from the City of God.

A prayer of someone depressed and fainting
A lament poured out before God

1 Adonai, hear my prayer,
   let my cry for help reach you;
2 do not hide your face from me
     when I am in trouble;
   turn your ear to me,
     when I call, be quick to answer me!
3 For my days are vanishing like smoke,
     my bones smoulder like logs,
4 my heart is withering like grass in the scorching sun
     and Death is consuming me;
5 whenever I heave a sigh,
     my bones stick through my skin.
6 I have become a vulture roaming the wilderness;
     a screech owl living in the ruins—
7 I lie awake lamenting,
     like a lone bird that chatters to itself on the roof.
8 My enemies taunt me all day long;
     those who used to praise me
     now use my name as a curse.
9 Ashes are the bread I eat,
     and everything I drink is laced with tears.
10 In your fury and your wrath,
     you picked me up only to toss me aside;
11 my days fade away like a shadow,
     and I am as dry as hay.

12 But you, Adonai, sit enthroned,
     and your renown lasts from one generation to the next!
13 Arise, and take pity on Zion!
     The time has come to have mercy on it,
     indeed, the hour has come;
14 for your faithful ones prize its stones
     and are moved to pity by its dust.
15 The nations revere your Name, Adonai,
     and all rulers of the earth stand in awe of your glory.
16 When you build Zion anew,
     your glory will be revealed;

17 Adonai, you will answer the prayer of the abandoned,
    and will not scorn their petitions.
18 Put this on record for the next generation,
    so that a people not yet born can praise Our God:
19 "Adonai has leaned down
    from the sanctuary on high,
    has looked down at earth from heaven,
20 to hear the groans of the captive,
    and to set free those condemned to death."
21 So the Name of Our God will be proclaimed in Zion
    and God's praise in Jerusalem;
22 nations and realms will be united
    and offer worship to Our God together.

23 You've broken my strength in mid-course,
    you have shortened my days.
24 Don't take me before my time,
    when your own life lasts forever!
25 Aeons ago you laid the earth's foundations,
    and the heavens are the work of your hands;
26 yet they will vanish, while you remain—
    they'll all wear out like a garment,
you'll change them like clothing,
    and then toss them away.
27 But you never change,
    and your years are unending.
28 The children of your faithful ones
    will have a permanent home,
and their descendants will be
    in your presence always.

1. Bless Adonai, my soul!
   All that is in me, bless God's holy Name!
2. Bless Adonai, my soul,
   and remember all God's kindnesses!
3. The One who forgives all your sins
   is the One who heals all your diseases;
4. the One who ransoms your life from the Pit
   is the One who crowns you with love and tenderness.
5. The One who fills your years with prosperity
   also gives you an eagle's youthful energy.

6. How you love justice, Adonai!
   You are always on the side of the oppressed.
7. You revealed your intentions to Moses,
   your deeds to Israel.
8. You are tender and compassionate, Adonai—
   slow to anger, and always loving;
9. your indignation doesn't endure forever,
   and your anger lasts only for a short time.
10. You never treat us as our sins deserve;
    you don't repay us in kind for the injustices we do.
11. For as high as heaven is above the earth,
    so great is the love for those who revere you.
12. As far away as the east is from the west,
    that's how far you remove our sins from us!
13. As tenderly as parents treat their children,
    that's how tenderly you treat your worshipers, Adonai!
14. For you know what we are made of—
    you remember that we're nothing but dust.
15. We last no longer than grass,
    live no longer than a wildflower;
16. one gust of wind and we're gone,
    never to be seen again.
17. Yet your love lasts from age to age
    for those who revere you, Adonai,
    as does your goodness to our children's children,
18. and to those who keep your Covenant
    and remember to obey your precepts.

¹⁹ You have established your judgment seat in the heavens,
   and your reign extends over everything.

²⁰ Bless Our God, you angels,
   you powers who do God's bidding,
   attentive to every word of command!
²¹ Bless Our God, you heavenly host,
   you faithful ones who enforce God's will!
²² Bless Our God, all creation,
   to the far reaches of God's reign!
   Bless Adonai, my soul!

1 Bless Our God, my soul!
   Adonai, my God, how great you are!
   Clothed in majesty and glory,
2   wrapped in a robe of light,
   you stretch the heavens out like a tent.
3 You lay the beams for your palace on the waters above;
   you use the clouds as your chariot
   and ride on the wings of the wind;
4 you use the winds as messengers
   and fiery flames as attendants.
5 You fixed the earth on its foundations
   so it can never totter,
6 and wrapped it with the Deep as with a robe,
   the waters overtopping the mountains.
7 At your rebuke the waters bolted,
   fleeing at the sound of your thunder,
8 cascading over the mountains, into the valleys,
   down to the reservoir you made for them;
9 you imposed boundaries they must never cross
   so they would never again flood the land.
10 You set springs gushing in ravines,
   running down between the mountains,
11 supplying water for wild animals
   and attracting the thirsty wild donkeys;
12 the birds of the air make their nests by these waters
   and sing among the branches.
13 From your palace you water the highlands
   until the ground is sated by the fruit of your work;
14 you make fresh grass grow for cattle
   and plants for us to cultivate
   to get food from the soil—
15 wine to cheer our hearts,
   oil to make our faces shine,
   and bread to sustain our life.
16 The trees of Our God drink their fill—
   those cedars of Lebanon,
17 where birds build their nests
   and, on the highest branches, the stork makes its home.

18 For the wild goats there are the high mountains,
    and in the crags the rock badgers hide.
19 You made the moon to tell the seasons,
    and the sun knows when to set:
20 you bring darkness on, night falls,
    and all the forest animals come out—
21 savage lions roaring for their prey,
    claiming their food from God.
22 The sun rises, they retire,
    going back to lie down in their lairs,
23 and people go out to work,
    to labor again until evening.
24 Adonai, what variety you have created,
    arranging everything so wisely!
    The earth is filled with your creativity!
25 There's the vast expanse of the Sea,
    teeming with countless creatures,
    living things large and small,
26 with the ships going to and fro
    and Leviathan whom you made to frolic there.
27 All creatures depend on you
    to feed them at the proper time.
28 Give it to them—they gather it up.
    Open your hand—they are well satisfied.
29 Hide your face—they are terrified.
    Take away their breath—they die and return to dust.
30 Send back your breath—fresh life begins
    and you renew the face of the earth.
31 Glory forever to Our God!
    May you find joy in your creation!
32 You glance at the earth and it trembles,
    you touch the mountains and they smoke!

33 I will sing to you all my life,
    I will make music for my God as long as I live.
34 May these reflections of mine give God
    as much pleasure as God gives me!
35 May the corrupt vanish from the earth
    and the violent exist no longer!
Bless Our God, my soul!
    Alleluia!

1 Alleluia!
Give thanks to Our God,
 and call on God's Name;
 proclaim God's deeds among the peoples!
2 Sing to God, sing praise,
 and tell of all God's marvels!
3 Glory in God's holy Name;
 let the hearts that seek Our God rejoice!
4 Turn to Our God—to God's strength—
 and seek God's presence constantly.
5 Remember the marvels God has done—
 the wonders performed and the judgments pronounced—
6 you descendants of Sarah and Abraham,
 God's faithful ones,
7 you offspring of Leah, Rachel and Jacob,
 who are God's chosen.
Adonai is our God,
 whose authority covers all the earth.

8 God remembers the Covenant forever,
 the promise God made for a thousand generations,
9 the pact made with Sarah and Abraham,
 the oath to Rebecca and Isaac,
10 the decree confirmed to Leah, Rachel and Jacob,
 an everlasting covenant for Israel.
11 "I give you the land of Canaan," said God,
 "as the portion you will inherit."
12 There they were fewer in number,
 no more than a handful, strangers to the country.
13 They roamed from nation to nation,
 from one land to another;
14 God let no one oppress them,
 and punished rulers on their behalf.
15 "Do not touch my anointed ones!" God said,
 "Do not harm my prophets!"
16 God called down a famine on the country
 and destroyed their supply of food.

17 Then God sent Joseph ahead of them,
    to be sold as a slave.
18 They put shackles on his feet,
    and placed an iron collar around his neck,
19 until Joseph's prophecy came to pass,
    and the word of Our God proved him true.
20 Pharaoh gave orders to release him;
    the ruler of Egypt set him free
21 and made him head of the royal household,
    and placed him in charge of the imperial treasury:
22 Joseph was to discipline the officials as he saw fit
    and to teach the elders wisdom.

23 Then Israel migrated to Egypt,
    and settled in the land of Ham.
24 Our God made the people fertile
    and more numerous than their oppressors,
25 whose hearts were turned to detest God's people
    and to conspire against God's faithful.
26 God sent Moses, Miriam and Aaron,
    God's faithful chosen ones,
27 and they performed God's miraculous signs among them—
    God's wonders in the land of Ham.
28 God sent darkness and darkness fell—
    for hadn't they defied God's word?
29 God turned their rivers into blood,
    which killed all their fish.
30 Their country was overrun with frogs,
    even in the Pharaoh's bedroom;
31 God spoke, and swarms of flies appeared,
    and clouds of mosquitoes infested the whole country.
32 God sent them hail instead of rain,
    and lightning across their land;
33 God leveled their vines and fig trees,
    and splintered the trees of their country.
34 God spoke and there came locusts and grasshoppers,
    more than you could count,
35 eating every green thing in the land,
    every blade their soil produced.
36 Then God struck down all the firstborn in the land,
    the entire firstfruits of their posterity;

37 and led Israel out with silver and gold,
   and not one among their tribes was left behind.
38 Egypt was glad to see them go,
   for Israel had filled them with dread.
39 God spread a cloud to cover them,
   and a fire to give light at night.
40 They demanded food, and God sent them quail
   and satisfied them with the bread of heaven;
41 God opened the rock, and waters gushed out,
   flowing through the desert like a river.
42 Yes, faithful to the sacred promise
   given to Sarah and Abraham,
43 God led the people out joyfully,
   singing their glad songs,
44 and gave them the lands of the nations.
   Where others had toiled, they took possession,
45 on condition that they kept God's statutes
   and obeyed the Laws.
   Alleluia!

1 Alleluia!
  Give thanks for Adonai's goodness;
    God's love endures forever!
2 Who can proclaim the mighty deeds of Our God,
    or show forth enough praise?
3 Happy are those who act justly,
    who do what is right always!
4 Remember me, Adonai,
    when you show favor to your people.
  Help me when you deliver them,
5   that I may enjoy the prosperity of your chosen ones,
  share the joy of your nation,
    and join with your own people in giving praise.

6 We have sinned the way our forebears did;
    gone astray and given in to corruption.
7 Our ancestors, when they were in Egypt,
    didn't perceive your wondrous works,
  didn't remember your abundant love,
    but there by the sea, by the Sea of Reeds, they rebelled.
8 Yet you saved them, O God, for the sake of your Name,
    to make your mighty power known.
9 You rebuked the Sea of Reeds, and it became dry;
    you led them through the deep as if it were a desert.
10 So God saved them from the hand of the adversary,
    delivered them from the power of the enemy.
11 The waters covered their foes,
    and not one of them was left.
12 Then they believed your promises
    and sang your praise.
13 But they soon forgot your works,
    would not wait to learn your plan,
14 and gave in to their craving in the wilderness,
    putting you to the test in the wasteland;
15 so you gave them what they asked for,
    then sent a wasting disease among them.
16 In the camp they grew jealous of
    Moses, Miriam and Aaron, your holy ones,

¹⁷ so the earth opened up and swallowed Dathan,
and buried the followers of Abiram.
¹⁸ Fire broke out among their throng,
a flame that consumed these corrupt people.
¹⁹ At Horeb they made a calf
and worshiped a molten image.
²⁰ They exchanged your glory
for the image of an ox that eats grass.
²¹ They forgot you, their Liberator,
who had done such great things in Egypt,
²² wondrous works in the land of Ham,
and awe-inspiring deeds at the Sea of Reeds.
²³ You would have destroyed them,
but Moses, your chosen one,
stood in the breach before you
and averted your destructive wrath.
²⁴ Then they despised the pleasant land,
and did not believe your promise.
²⁵ They grumbled in their tents,
and did not obey your voice.
²⁶ So you swore with upraised hand
that they would fall in the wilderness,
²⁷ and their descendants would be dispersed among the nations,
scattered throughout the lands.
²⁸ Then they attached themselves to the Baal of Peor,
and ate sacrifices offered to lifeless gods;
²⁹ they provoked you to anger with their doings,
and a plague broke out among them.
³⁰ Then Phinehas stood up and intervened,
and the plague was stopped—
³¹ and it has been remembered as a just act
from generation to generation forever.
³² They angered you at the waters of Meribah,
and Moses suffered on their account;
³³ for they rebelled against your Spirit
and Moses spoke rashly.
³⁴ They did not destroy the peoples
as you had commanded them,
³⁵ but they mingled with the nations
and learned to do as they did.
³⁶ They worshiped their idols,
which became a snare to them.

37 They sacrificed their own children,
    sacrificed them to demons;
38 they shed innocent blood,
    the blood of their children,
  whom they sacrificed to the idols of Canaan;
    and the land was polluted with blood.
39 Thus they became unclean by their acts,
    and debauched by their deeds.
40 Therefore, you became angry with your people
    and you abhorred your inheritance,
41 and handed them over to the nations,
    so that their enemies ruled over them.
42 Their foes oppressed them,
    and subjected them to their power.
43 You delivered them again and again,
    but they were willfully rebellious,
    and were brought low through their sin.
44 But when you heard their cry
    you saw that they were in distress;
45 you remembered your Covenant for their sake
    and out of your great love, relented.
46 You made all their captors
    take pity on them.

47 Save us, Adonai, our God,
    and gather us from among the nations,
  that we may give thanks to your holy Name
    and glory in your praise!

48 Blessed be Our God, the God of Israel,
    from everlasting to everlasting!
  And let all the people say,
    "Amen, alleluia!"

book v

1 "Give thanks for Adonai's goodness;
   God's love endures forever!"
2 Let these be the words of Adonai's redeemed,
   those redeemed from the oppressor's clutches,
3 those brought home from foreign lands,
   from east and west, from northern lands and southern seas.

4 Some lost their way in the wilderness, in the wasteland,
   not knowing how to reach an inhabited town;
5 they were hungry and thirsty,
   and their courage was running low.
6 They called to Our God in their trouble,
   and God rescued them from their sufferings,
7 guiding them by a direct route
   to an inhabited town.
8 Let them thank Adonai for this great love,
   for the marvels done for all people—
9 for God has satisfied the thirsty
   and filled the hungry with good things.

10 Some were living in gloom and darkness,
   prisoners suffering in iron chains
11 because they defied God's word,
   and scorned the advice of the Most High.
12 God humbled their hearts with suffering;
   they stumbled and there was no one to help them.
13 Then they called to Our God in their trouble
   and God rescued them from their sufferings,

14 releasing them from gloom and darkness
   and shattering their chains.
15 Let them thank Adonai for this great love,
   for the marvels done for all people—
16 for breaking bronze gates open
   and smashing iron bars.

17 Some were fools who suffered because of their rebellion,
   because of their own sins,
18 until they were so sick, nearly at death's door,
   that food became repugnant.
19 Then they called to Our God in their trouble
   and God rescued them from their sufferings,
20 sending a word to heal them,
   and snatching them from the Pit.
21 Let them thank Adonai for this great love,
   for the marvels done for all people.
22 Let them offer sacrifices of thanksgiving
   and recount what God has done in joyful song.

23 Some went down to the sea in ships,
   plying their trade across the ocean;
24 they too saw the works of Our God,
   the wonders that God worked on the Deep!
25 God spoke and raised a storm wind,
   lashing up towering waves.
26 Flung to the sky, then plunged to the depths,
   in the ordeal their courage melted away.
27 They staggered and reeled like drunkards
   with all their skill adrift.
28 Then they called to Our God in their trouble,
   and God rescued them from their sufferings,
29 reducing the storm to a whisper
   until the waves of the sea were hushed;
30 overjoyed with the calm,
   they were brought safe to the port they were bound for.
31 Let them thank God for this great love,
   for the marvels done for all people.
32 Let them praise God in the Great Assembly
   and give praise in the Council of Elders.

33 Sometimes God turned rivers into desert,
   springs of water into arid ground,
34 or a fertile country into salt flats,
   because the people living there were corrupt.
35 So God would turn desert into pools of water,
   or an arid country into flowing springs
36 to give the hungry a home,
   a place to build and call their own.
37 There they sow fields and plant vineyards
   that yield a plentiful harvest.
38 God blesses them, their numbers grow,
   and their livestock never decrease.
39 Or their numbers dwindle,
   with oppression, disaster and hardship taking their toll.
40 God pours contempt upon the nobly born
   and leaves them to wander in trackless wastes,
41 but lifts the needy out of their misery,
   and increases their families like flocks.

42 The upright see it and rejoice,
   but all wrongdoers shut their mouths.
43 If you are wise, study these things
   and realize the great love of Our God.

1 My heart is ready, Adonai,
      and I will sing, sing your praise,
      with all my heart.
2 Awake, lyre and harp—
      I will wake the dawn!
3 I will thank you, Adonai, among the peoples,
      among the nations I will praise you,
4 for your love reaches to the heavens
      and your truth to the skies.
5 Adonai, go even higher than the heavens,
      and let your glory be over the earth
6   so that those you love will be delivered!
   Let your right hand become our deliverance
      and answer me!

7 From the holy place God has made this promise:
   "In my joy I wiil apportion Shechem
      and measure out the valley of Succoth.
8 Gilead is mine,
      and Manasseh is mine as well.
    Ephraim I take for my helmet,
      Judah for my scepter.
9 Moab I will use for my washbowl,
      on Edom I will plant my shoe;
      and over Philistia I will shout in triumph."

10 But who will lead me to conquer the fortress?
      Who will bring me face to face with Edom?
11 Will you completely reject us, Adonai,
      and no longer march with us?
12 Give us help against the enemy,
      for our own power is useless.
13 With you we will fight valiantly,
      and it is you who will trample our foes.

For the conductor
A psalm of David

1 O God of my praise,
     break your silence,

2 now that the corrupt and the deceitful
     are accusing and defaming me,

3 saying malicious things about me,
     attacking me for no reason.

4 In return for my friendship, they denounce me,
     though all I had done was pray for them;

5 they have repaid my kindness with evil,
     my love with hatred.

6 Let *them* stand before a corrupt judge,
     and let *them* be framed with false accusations;

7 when they are judged, make sure they are found guilty,
     and let their prayer be construed as a crime!

8 Let their life be cut short
     and let someone else take their office;

9 let their children be orphaned
     and their spouses bereft!

10 Let their children be homeless beggars,
     searching for food far from their ruined homes;

11 let their creditors seize their possessions
     and foreigners swallow their profits!

12 Let no one be left to show them kindness,
     let no one look after their orphans!

13 Let their family die out,
     their name disappear in one generation!

14 Let the crimes of their ancestors
     be held against them before God,
     and their parents' sins never be erased;

15 let Our God bear them constantly in mind,
     and wipe their memory from the earth!

16 They never thought of being kind,
     but persecuted the poor, the needy and the brokenhearted
     and hounded them to death.

17 They loved pronouncing curses, so curses came to them gladly;
     they had no taste for blessing, so it will shun them.

18 They wrapped themselves up in their curses,
    which soaked right into them like water,
    deep into their bones like oil—
19 and now those same curses envelop them like a cloak,
    belted around their waists forever.
20 This is the way God will repay all my accusers,
    all who speak evil against me!

21 Adonai, defend me for the sake of your Name,
    rescue me in the generosity of your love!
22 Reduced to affliction and poverty,
    my heart is wounded within me.
23 I am dwindling away like a shadow,
    I have been shaken off like a locust.
24 My knees are weak for lack of food,
    my body is thin and gaunt;
25 I have become an object of derision;
    people shake their heads when they see me.
26 Help me, Adonai, my God,
    save me because of your love!
27 Let them know that this is your hand,
    that it was you, Adonai, who has done all this.
28 Counter their curses with your blessing,
    shame my aggressors when they arise,
    and make your faithful one glad!
29 Clothe my accusers in disgrace,
    cover them with a cloak of their own shame.

30 I will give thanks aloud to Our God,
    and proclaim God's praise in the Assembly—
31 for taking the side of poor people,
    defending them against those
    who would sentence them to death.

110

A psalm of David

1 Our God said to my Sovereign One:
"Sit at my right hand,
until I make your enemies your footstool."
2 Adonai, stretch forth your mighty scepter from Zion,
and rule in the midst of your enemies!
3 Your people will offer themselves freely
on the day you lead your host
upon the holy mountains.
From the womb of the morning
your young people will come to you, plentiful as the dew.
4 Our God has sworn and will not retract:
"You are a priest forever
in the line of Melchizedek."
5 With God at your side
you will shatter rulers on the day of wrath.
6 You will execute judgment among the nations,
filling them with corpses;
you will shatter chiefs over the wide earth.
7 And because you will drink from the brook along the way,
you will be strengthened and victorious!

1 Alleluia!
   I will thank you, Adonai, with all my heart
   in the meeting of the just and their assembly.
2 Great are your works,
   to be pondered by all who love them.
3 Majestic and glorious are your works,
   and your justice stands firm forever.
4 You make us remember your wonders—
   you are compassion and love.
5 You give food to those who revere you,
   keeping your Covenant ever in mind.
6 You reveal to your people the power of your actions
   by giving them the lands of the nations as their inheritance.
7 The works of your hands are truth and justice,
   and all your precepts are sure,
8 standing firm forever and ever,
   and carried out uprightly and faithfully.
9 You have sent deliverance to your people
   and established your Covenant forever.
   Your Name is holy and awe-inspiring!
10 Reverence for Our God is the beginning of wisdom—
   and those who have it prove themselves wise.
   Your praise will last forever!

---

* This psalm is an acrostic poem: the first letter of each line begins with a subsequent letter of the Hebrew alphabet.

1   Alleluia!
    Happiness comes to those who revere Our God,
      who revel in God's commands!

2   Their children hold power on earth;
      the descendants of the just will always be blessed.

3   There will be riches and wealth for their families,
      and God's justice can never be changed.

4   For the just, Our God shines like a lamp in the dark,
      God is merciful, compassionate and righteous.

5   Good people are generous, and lend money without interest;
      they are honest in all their dealings.

6   They are never shaken, because they love justice
      and will leave an imperishable memory behind them.

7   They never fear bad news,
      because their unwavering hearts trust in Our God.

8   With peaceful hearts, they fear nothing;
      and in the end they will triumph over their enemies.

9   Quick to be generous, they give to the poor,
      doing justice always and forever;
      their horn will always be lifted in honor.

10   The corrupt become infuriated when they see this;
      they grind their teeth and waste away,
      finally vanishing like their empty dreams.

---

* This psalm is an acrostic poem: the first letter of each line begins with a subsequent letter of the Hebrew alphabet.

113

1 Alleluia!
  You faithful of Our God, give praise,
      praise the Name of Our God!
2 Blessed be the Name of Our God,
      from now and for all times!
3 From the rising of the sun to its setting,
      praised be the Name of Our God!
4 You are high over all nations, Adonai!
      Your glory transcends the heavens!
5 Who is like you, Adonai, our God?
      Enthroned so high,
6 you need to stoop
      to see the sky and the earth!
7 You raise the poor from the dust,
      and lift the needy from the dung heap
8 to give them a place at the table with rulers,
      with the leaders of your people.
9 You give the childless couple a home
      filled with the joy of many children.
  Alleluia!

1 Alleluia!
   When Israel came out of Egypt,
     from a people who spoke an alien tongue,
2 Judah became God's Temple,
     Israel became God's domain.
3 The sea fled at the sight:
     the Jordan turned back on its course,
4 the mountains leapt like rams,
     and the hills like yearling sheep.
5 Why was it, sea, that you fled—
     that you turned back, Jordan, on your course?
6 Mountains, why did you leap like rams—
     you hills, like yearling sheep?
7 Earth, tremble before your Maker,
     before the God of Israel,
8 who turned the rock into a pool of water
     and flint into a bubbling fountain!

1 Not to us, Adonai, not to us,
     but to your Name give the glory
     for the sake of your love and faithfulness.
2 Why do the nations say,
     "Where is their God?"
3 But you, Adonai, are in the heavens,
     doing whatever you will.
4 Their idols are silver and gold,
     the work of human hands.
5 These "gods" have mouths but they cannot speak;
     they have eyes but they cannot see;
6 they have ears but they cannot hear;
     they have noses but they cannot smell.

7 They have hands but they cannot feel;
    they have feet but they cannot walk—
    and no sound comes from their throats.
8 Their makers will become just like them,
    and so will all who trust in them!

9 Descendants of Israel, trust in Our God,
    who is your help and your shield.
10 Daughters of Miriam, Sons of Aaron, trust in Our God,
    who is your help and your shield.
11 You who revere Adonai, trust in Our God,
    who is your help and your shield.

12 Our God remembers us and blesses us;
    Our God will bless the children of Israel,
    the children of the Covenant.
13 Those who revere Our God will be blessed,
    the humble no less than the great;
14 may Our God increase you,
    you and all your children.
15 May you be blessed by Our God,
    who made heaven and earth!
16 The heavens, the heavens belong to Our God,
    but the earth God has given to humankind.
17 The dead will not praise Our God,
    nor those who go down into silence.
18 But we who live bless Our God,
    now and forever.
    Alleluia!

116

1 I love you, Adonai, for you have heard
    my cry for mercy.
2 You have listened to me;
    I will call on you all my days.

3 The bands of Death encircled me;
   the messengers of Sheol ambushed me,
   I was overcome with trouble and sorrow.
4 Then I called your Name, Adonai—
   "Help, Adonai, save me!"

5 You are gracious, Adonai, and just;
   Our God is compassionate.
6 You protect those without guile;
   when I was brought low, you saved me.
7 Be at rest once again, my soul,
   for Our God has been good to you.
8 You have rescued my soul from Death,
   my eyes from Tears,
   and my feet from Banishment.
9 I walk before you, Adonai,
   in the land of the living.
10 I believed even when I said,
   "I am completely crushed,"
11 and in despair said,
   "No one can be trusted."

12 How can I repay you, Adonai,
   for all your goodness to me?
13 I raise the cup of deliverance,
   and call on the Name of Our God.
14 I will fulfill my vows to you
   in the presence of all your people.
15 The death of your faithful
   is precious in your sight.
16 Adonai, I am your faithful one—
   I am faithful to you alone,
   the child of your fidelity.
   You have freed me from my chains.
17 I will offer you the sacrifice of praise,
   and call on the Name of Our God.
18 I will fulfill my vows to you
   in the presence of all your people,
19 in the courts of the house of Our God,
   in the midst of Jerusalem.
   Alleluia!

117

1 Praise Our God, all you nations,
    extol God, all you mighty ones.
2 For God's love toward us is great,
    God's faithfulness, eternal.
  Alleluia!

118

1 I thank you, Adonai, for your goodness!
    Your love is everlasting!
2 Let Israel say it:
    "Your love is everlasting!"
3 Let the House of Aaron say it:
    "Your love is everlasting!"
4 Let those who revere Our God say it:
    "Your love is everlasting!"

5 In anguish, I cried to you, Adonai,
    and you answered me with freedom.
6 Because Our God is with me, I'm not afraid—
    what can anyone do to me?
7 Because Our God is with me as my Helper,
    I can triumph over my enemies.
8 Better to take refuge in Our God
    than to trust in human beings;
9 better to take refuge in Our God
    than to follow leaders.
10 The nations were swarming round me,
    but I stood my ground in the Name of Our God.
11 They swarmed round me closer and closer,
    but I stood my ground in the Name of Our God;
12 They swarmed round me like bees,
    but they died like thorns in a bonfire;
    I stood my ground in the Name of Our God.

13 I was pressed, pressed, about to fall,
     but Our God came to my help.

14 God is my strength and my song;
     God has become my salvation!
15 Raise shouts of joy and victory
     in the tents of the upright:
     Our God's right hand is doing mighty acts!
16 Our God's right hand is winning,
     Our God's right hand is doing mighty acts!
17 No, I will not die—
     I will live to proclaim the deeds of Our God;
18 though Our God has disciplined me often,
     I am not abandoned to Death.
19 Open the gates of justice for me,
     let me come in and thank you, Adonai!
20 This is the gate of Our God,
     and only the upright can enter!
21 Thank you for hearing me,
     for saving me.
22 It was the stone which the builders rejected
     that became the keystone;
23 this is Our God's doing,
     and it is wonderful to see.
24 This is the day Our God has made—
     let us celebrate with joy!

25 Please, Adonai, please save us!
     Please, Adonai, give us prosperity now!
26. Blessings on the one who comes in the Name of Our God!
     We bless you from Adonai's Temple!
27 Adonai is God
     and God has enlightened us.
   Join the festal procession!
     With palm fronds in hand, go up to the horns of the altar!
28 You are my God, and I thank you;
     you are my God, and I exalt you.
   Thank you for hearing me,
     for saving me.
29 Thank you, Adonai, for your goodness!
     Your love is everlasting!

aleph

1 Happiness comes to those whose way is blameless,
   who walk in your Law, Adonai.
2 Happiness comes to those who keep your decrees,
   and seek you with all their heart,
3 and do no wrong,
   but walk in your ways.
4 You have commanded that your precepts
   be kept diligently—
5 if only I were more faithful
   in keeping your statutes!
6 Then I wouldn't feel so ashamed
   when I look at all your commands.
7 I will thank you with an upright heart,
   when I truly learn to be as just as you want me to be.
8 I will obey your statutes;
   do not utterly forsake me.

beth

9 How can young people keep themselves
   on the straight and narrow?
   By keeping to your words!
10 With all my heart I seek you;
    let me not stray from your commands.
11 In my heart I treasure your promise
    so that I keep from sinning against you.
12 Blessed are you, Adonai—
    teach me your statutes!
13 With my lips I declare
    every ordinance you've spoken.
14 I rejoice in the path you decree
    as much as I'd rejoice in great wealth.
15 I meditate on your precepts
    and ponder your ways.

---

* This psalm is an acrostic poem: the first word of each stanza begins with a subsequent letter of the Hebrew alphabet.

16 I delight in your statutes;
    I will not forget your words.

ghimel

17 Be good to your faithful one,
    that I may live and keep your words.
18 Open my eyes, and let me ponder
    the wonders of your Law.
19 No matter where I am on earth, I am a foreigner;
    don't hide your commands from me.
20 I am eaten up with longing
    for your ordinances all the time.
21 You rebuke the arrogant with a curse,
    for turning away from your commands.
22 Take scorn and contempt away from me,
    for I keep your decrees.
23 Though tyrants conspire and testify against me,
    your faithful one meditates on your statutes.
24 Yes, your decrees are my delight—
    they are my counselors.

daleth

25 Down in the dust I lie;
    give me life according to your word.
26 I was honest about my past ways, and you answered me;
    teach me your statutes.
27 Make me understand the way of your precepts,
    and I will meditate on your wondrous deeds.
28 My soul is weary with sorrow;
    strengthen me according to your word.
29 Keep me from the habit of telling lies,
    and give me grace through your Law.
30 I choose the path of truth;
    I have set my heart on your ordinances.
31 I cling to your decrees;
    Adonai, don't let me be ashamed.
32 I will run headlong down the road of your commands,
    for you have set my heart free.

he

33 Educate me, Adonai, in the way of your statutes,
   and I'll keep them to the end.
34 Give me discernment, that I may observe your Law
   and obey it with all my heart.
35 Lead me in the path of your commands—
   that is where I'll find joy.
36 Draw my heart to your decrees
   and not toward selfish gain.
37 Turn my eyes away from looking at worthless things;
   make me alive in your way.
38 Fulfill for your faithful
   your promise to those who fear you.
39 Take away the reproach which I dread,
   for your ordinances are good.
40 See how I long for your precepts!
   In your justice give me life.

waw

41 Fulfill your promise, Adonai,
   and let your love, your salvation come to me.
42 Then I'll have a word for those who taunt me,
   for it is *your* word that I trust.
43 Don't steal the word of truth from my mouth completely;
   for I put my hope in your ordinances.
44 And I will obey your Law continually,
   forever and ever.
45 I will walk in freedom,
   because I seek your precepts.
46 I will speak of your decrees before heads of state,
   and I will not be ashamed.
47 I delight in your commands,
   because I love them.
48 I will lift up my hands to your commands because I love them,
   and I'll meditate on your statutes.

zayin

49 Grant to your faithful one the fulfillment of your word,
   for you have given me hope.
50 Your life-giving promise
   has been great comfort during my torment.

51 Though the proud scoff bitterly at me,
   I do not turn away from your Law.
52 I remember your ancient ordinances, Adonai,
   and I am comforted.
53 Indignation seizes me
   because of the corrupt who reject your Law.
54 Your statutes are all I sing about
   in my wayfarer's shelter.
55 I remember you in the night, Adonai,
   and I will keep your Law.
56 For it has been my fortune
   to obey your precepts.

heth

57 Did I not say, Adonai, that my role
   is to keep your words?
58 I sought your face with all my heart;
   give me grace, as you promised.
59 I examined my own ways,
   and turned my feet to your decrees.
60 I'll be prompt and will not hesitate
   in keeping your commands.
61 Though the ropes of violent people bind me hand and foot,
   I won't forget your Law.
62 When I wake up in the middle of the night
   I thank you for your just ordinances.
63 I am a friend to all who revere you
   and keep your precepts.
64 Your love, Adonai, fills the earth;
   teach me your statutes!

teth

65 In keeping with your promise,
   do good to your faithful one.
66 Give me insight and understanding,
   for I trust in your commands.
67 Before I was disciplined I went astray,
   but now I obey your word.
68 You are good and what you do is good;
   teach me your statutes.
69 Though arrogant people smear me with lies,
   I observe your precepts with all my heart.

⁷⁰ Their heart has become calloused and bloated,
    but I delight in your Law.
⁷¹ It was good for me to have been afflicted,
    because through it I learned your statutes.
⁷² The law of your mouth is more precious to me
    than gold and silver coins by the thousands.

yod

⁷³ Just as your hands made me and shaped me,
    give me discernment, that I may learn your commands.
⁷⁴ Those who revere you will rejoice when they see me,
    because I hope in your word.
⁷⁵ I know, Adonai, that your ordinances are just,
    and that you afflicted me only because of your faithfulness.
⁷⁶ Let your love comfort me now,
    as you promised your faithful one.
⁷⁷ Let your compassion come to me and breathe life back into me,
    for your Law is my delight.
⁷⁸ Let the arrogant be put to shame for oppressing me unjustly;
    as for me, I'll meditate on your precepts.
⁷⁹ Let those who revere you turn to me,
    those who acknowledge your decrees.
⁸⁰ Let my heart be perfect in your statutes,
    so that I will never be put to shame.

kaph

⁸¹ Keenly I long for your salvation;
    I hope in your word.
⁸² My eyes strain, looking for your promise—
    when will you comfort me?
⁸³ Though I'm as shriveled as an old withered wineskin,
    I have not forgotten your statutes.
⁸⁴ How long must your faithful one wait?
    When will you pass sentence on my persecutors?
⁸⁵ They have set their traps in my path,
    arrogantly ignoring your Law.
⁸⁶ But all your commands are trustworthy,
    and they persecute me without cause! Help me!
⁸⁷ They almost wiped me off the face of the earth,
    but I haven't forsaken your precepts.
⁸⁸ In your love, keep me alive,
    and I will obey everything you say.

lamed

89 Like the heavens in their constancy,
   your word, Adonai, endures forever.
90 Through one generation to the next, your faithfulness continues,
   as firmly established as the earth itself.
91 Your ordinances endure to this day
   for all who are faithful to you.
92 If your Law hadn't been my delight,
   I'd have been lost in my affliction.
93 I will never forget your precepts,
   for through them you gave me life.
94 I am yours—save me,
   for I have sought your precepts!
95 Violent people wait to destroy me,
   but I pay heed to your decrees.
96 Even perfection has its limits, I see—
   but your command is absolutely limitless.

mem

97 My meditation all day long is your Law—
   how I love it!
98 Your commands make me wiser than my enemies,
   for they are always with me.
99 I have more insight than all my teachers,
   for your decrees are my meditation.
100 I understand more than the elders,
   because I obey your precepts.
101 I've kept my feet from straying onto any evil path,
   so that I could obey your words.
102 I have never turned away from your ordinances,
   for you yourself have taught me.
103 How sweet is the taste of your promises—
   sweeter than honey in my mouth!
104 Through your precepts, I gain discernment,
   and because of them I hate every wrong path.

nun

105 Now I know your word is a lamp for my steps,
   for the path just ahead of me.
106 I resolve and swear
   to keep your ordinances of justice.

107 I have suffered much, Adonai—
　　give me life as you have promised.
108 Please accept my heartfelt praises, Adonai,
　　and teach me your decrees.
109 Though constantly I take my life in my hands,
　　I never forgot your Law.
110 The corrupt laid their traps for me,
　　but I haven't strayed from your precepts.
111 Your decrees are all the inheritance I'll ever want—
　　they're the joy of my heart.
112 I set my heart to keep your statutes,
　　forever and to the letter.

samekh

113 Oh, how I hate duplicitous people!
　　But I love your Law.
114 You are my refuge and my shield;
　　in your word I hope.
115 Get away from me, you reprobates,
　　so that I can keep the commands of my God!
116 Sustain me as you have promised, that I may live;
　　don't let me be ashamed for hoping in you.
117 Help me and I will be safe,
　　and forever delight in your statutes.
118 You reject all who stray from your statutes,
　　they know nothing but emptiness and deceit.
119 You sweep the corrupt away like a pile of ashes—
　　that is why I love your decrees.
120 My body trembles in awe of you,
　　and I revere your ordinances.

ayin

121 Please don't abandon me to my oppressors,
　　for I have done what is upright and just.
122 Ensure the well-being of your faithful one,
　　don't let the arrogant oppress me.
123 My eyes strain looking for your salvation
　　and your just promise.
124 Deal with your faithful one out of your love,
　　and teach me your statutes.
125 I am faithful to you;
　　give me discernment so that I can understand your decrees.

126 It's time to act, Adonai!
    They're breaking your Law!
127 That is why I love your commands more than gold,
    more than the purest gold.
128 This is why I trust all your precepts
    and hate every destructive path.

pe

129 Quite wonderful are your decrees—
    that is why I obey them.
130 The revelation of your words sheds light,
    giving understanding to the guileless.
131 I pant with open mouth
    in my longing for your commands.
132 Turn to me, have mercy on me,
    as you turn to those who love your Name.
133 Direct my footsteps as you promise,
    and don't let sin govern my life.
134 Ransom me from all oppression,
    that I can keep your precepts.
135 Let your face shine upon your faithful one,
    and teach me your statutes.
136 Streams of tears flow from my eyes
    because others do not obey your Law.

tsadhe

137 Righteous are you, Adonai,
    and your ordinance is just.
138 You have pronounced your decrees in justice
    and in perfect faithfulness.
139 My zeal consumes me
    because my foes forget your words.
140 Your promise is absolutely trustworthy,
    and your faithful one loves it.
141 I am lowly and contemptible,
    but I have never forgotten you.
142 Your justice is everlasting justice,
    and your Law is truth itself.
143 Though distress and anguish come upon me,
    your commands are my delight.
144 Your decrees are forever just;
    make me understand them, that I might live.

qoph

145 So I call out with all my heart—answer me, Adonai,
   and I will obey your statutes.
146 I call upon you—save me,
   and I will keep your decrees!
147 I wake before the dawn and cry out for help;
   I hope in your words.
148 My eyes greet the night watches
   in meditation on your promise.
149 Hear my voice because of your love, Adonai,
   and give me life through your ordinances.
150 Malicious schemers are near me,
   but they are far from your Law.
151 You, Adonai, are near,
   and all your commands endure forever.
152 Long ago I learned your decrees,
   and you planted them for all time.

resh

153 Behold my affliction, and rescue me,
   for I have not forgotten your Law.
154 Plead my cause and ransom me!
   Give me life, as you promised!
155 Deliverance is far from the corrupt
   because they don't seek your statutes.
156 Your compassion is great, Adonai,
   give me life, as your ordinances promise.
157 Though my persecutors and enemies are many,
   I haven't turned from your decrees.
158 I look upon the faithless with loathing,
   because they do not obey your word.
159 See how I love your precepts, Adonai!
   In your great love, give me life.
160 Your word is true above all else;
   all of your just ordinances are everlasting.

shin

161 Unjustly, I am persecuted by our leaders,
   but my heart stands in awe of your word.
162 I rejoice at your promise,
   like one who has found rich plunder.

163 I hate lies—I abhor them!
   But I love your Law.
164 Seven times a day I praise you
   for your just ordinances.
165 Those who love your Law have great peace,
   and for them there is no stumbling block.
166 I wait for your salvation, Adonai,
   and I follow your commands.
167 I keep your decrees
   and love them deeply.
168 I obey your precepts and decrees,
   for all my ways are before you.

taw

169 View my petition when it comes before you, Adonai;
   in keeping with your word give me discernment.
170 Let my supplication reach you;
   rescue me as you promised.
171 Let my lips pour forth your praise
   because you teach me your statutes.
172 Let my tongue sing of your promise,
   for all your commands are just.
173 Let your hand be ready to help me,
   for I have chosen your precepts.
174 I long for your salvation, Adonai,
   and your Law is my delight.
175 Let me live to praise you,
   and let your ordinances sustain me.
176 I've gone astray like a lost sheep—search for your faithful one,
   because I have never forgotten your commands.

the songs of ascents
psalms 120-134

120

A Song of Ascents

1 When I was in trouble, I called to you, Adonai,
    and you answered me.
2 Save me from these liars
    and from all these double-crossers!
3 What will God do to you, you foul liar?
    How will God punish you?
4 You'll be shot through with arrows,
    or burned with blazing coals!
5 Living among you is as bad as living in Mesech
    or among the people of Kedar!

6 I have lived too long
    with belligerent people!
7 I stand for peace,
    but when I talk of peace, they want war!

121

A Song of Ascents

1 I lift my eyes to the mountains—
    from where will my help come?
2 My help comes from Our God,
    who made heaven and earth!
3 Our God won't let our footsteps slip:
    our Guardian never sleeps.
4 The Guardian of Israel
    will never slumber, never sleep!

5   Our God is our Guardian,
     Our God is our shade:
  with God by our side,
6   the sun cannot overpower us by day,
     nor the moon at night.
7   Our God guards us from harm,
     guards our lives.
8   Our God guards our leaving and our coming back,
     now and forever.

122

A Song of Ascents
By David

1   How I rejoiced when they said to me,
     "Let us go to the house of Our God!"
2   And now our feet are standing
     within your gates, Jerusalem.
3   Jerusalem restored!
     The city, one united whole!
4   Here the tribes ascend,
     the tribes of Our God.
  They come to praise Our God's Name,
     as God commanded Israel—
5   here, where the tribunals of justice are,
     the judgment seats of David's house.
6   Pray for peace within Jerusalem:
     "May those who love you prosper!
7   May peace be in your walls!
     May your citadels be always secure!"
8   For the sake of my family and friends,
     I say, "Peace be within you!"
9   For the sake of Adonai our God,
     I will seek your good.

123

A Song of Ascents

1 I lift up my eyes to you,
     you who sit enthroned in the heavens!
2 As the eyes of a dog
       look to the hand of its owner—
   as the eyes of attendants
       look to the hand of those they serve—
3 so our eyes look to you, Adonai,
       until you show us your mercy!
4 Have mercy on us, Adonai, have mercy!
       We have endured so much contempt.
5 We have endured far too much
       ridicule from the wealthy,
       too much contempt from the arrogant!

124

A Song of Ascents
By David

1 "If it had not been Adonai who was on our side"—
       let Israel now say—
2 "if it had not been Adonai who was on our side,
       when enemies attacked us,
3   they'd have swallowed us alive!
   When their anger burned against us,
4   the flood would have swept us away,
   the water would have drowned us,
5   the raging torrent would have engulfed us!"

6 Blessed be Adonai,
       who has not let us fall prey to their teeth!
7 We are free like a bird from the trap!
       The snare has been broken and we are free!
8 Our help is in the Name of Adonai,
       who made heaven and earth.

1 Those who trust in you, Adonai,
   are like Mount Zion,
   which cannot be moved
   but endures forever.
2 As mountains surround Jerusalem
   so you surround your people,
   both now and forever more.
3 For the scepter of corruption won't last
   over the land allotted to the upright,
   to spare the upright from the temptation
   to use their hands for evil.

4 Do good, Adonai, to the good,
   to those who are upright in their hearts!
5 But those who turn aside on their crooked roads, Adonai,
   you will lead them away with the evildoers!
   Peace be upon Israel!

A Song of Ascents

1 When Our God brought us captives back to Zion,
       we thought we were dreaming!
2 Our mouths were filled with laughter then,
       our tongues with songs of joy.
   And from the nations we heard,
       "Their God has done great things for them."
3 Yes—Our God has done great things for us,
       and we are filled with joy.

4 Now set our captive hearts free, Adonai!
       Make them like streams in the driest desert!
5 Then those who now sow in tears
       will reap with shouts of joy;
6 those who go out weeping as they
       carry their seed for sowing,
   will come back with shouts of joy
       as they carry their harvest home.

A Song of Ascents
By Solomon

1 If Our God doesn't build the house,
       the builders work in vain;
   if Our God doesn't guard the city,
       the sentries watch in vain.
2 In vain you get up early and stay up late,
       sweating to make a living,
   because God loves us and provides for us
       even while we sleep.

3   Children are the heritage God gives us;
      our descendants are our rewards.
4   Having children when you are young
      is like equipping an archer with wonderful new arrows.
    Happy are those who have filled their quiver
      with such arrows!
    When they argue with their enemies at the city gate,
      no one will be able to make them feel ashamed.

128

A Song of Ascents

1   Happiness comes to those who revere Our God,
      and walk in God's ways!
2   You will eat what your hands have worked for;
      you will be blessed and prosperous.
3   You will be a fruitful vine
      in the heart of your house;
    your children will grow up around your table,
      spring up like olive trees.
4   This is how you will be blessed
      if you revere Our God.
5   May Our God bless you from Zion,
      and may you see the prosperity of Jerusalem
      all the days of your life!
6   May you live to see your children's children!
      Peace be on Israel!

129

1 "They have oppressed me continually ever since I was a child"—
     let Israel now say—
2 "they've oppressed me continually ever since I was a child,
     but they have never been victorious over me!
3 My back looks like a plowed field—
     the furrows are long and deep.
4 But the God of Justice has severed
     the cords of the tyrant!"

5 Let all who hate Zion be put to shame,
     be turned away.
6 Let them be like the grass on our flat clay housetops—
     it withers in the heat before you can pluck it,
7 so sparse that there's not a handful for the reaper,
     nothing for the gatherer to carry away.
8 Let no one who walks past them ever say,
     "The blessing of God be upon you!
     We bless you in the Name of Our God!"

130

A Song of Ascents

1 Out of the depths I cry to you, Adonai!
2   God, hear my voice!
   Let your ears be attentive
     to my voice, my cries for mercy!
3 If you kept track of our sins, Adonai,
     who could stand before you?
4 But with you is forgiveness,
     and for this we revere you.

⁵ So I wait for you, Adonai—
   my soul waits,
   and in your word I place my trust.
⁶ My soul longs for you, Adonai,
   more than sentinels long for the dawn,
   more than sentinels long for the dawn.
⁷ Israel, put your hope in Our God,
   for with Adonai is abundant love
   and the fullness of deliverance;
⁸ God will deliver Israel
   from all its failings.

131

A Song of Ascents
By David

¹ Adonai, my heart has no lofty ambitions,
   my eyes don't look too high.
   I am not concerned with great affairs
   or marvels beyond my scope.
² It's enough for me to keep my soul tranquil
   and quiet like a child in its mother's arms;
   my soul is as content as a nursing child.
³ Israel, rely on Our God like a child,
   now and forever!

1   O God, remember David
       and all his hardships!
2   Remember the oath he swore to you,
       his vow to the Strong One of Israel:
3   "I won't enter my house,
       I won't go to my bed—
4   I won't give sleep to my eyes
       or slumber to my eyelids
5   until I find a place for Our God,
       a dwelling for the Strong One of Israel!"
6   At Ephrata we heard of the ark;
       we found it on the plains of Yearim.
7   Let us go then, to the place of God's dwelling;
       let us kneel at Our God's footstool.
8   Arise, Adonai, to the place of your rest,
       you and the ark of your strength!
9   Your priests will be clothed with holiness;
       your faithful will sing for joy.

10 For the sake of David, your faithful one,
       don't reject your Anointed.
11 You swore an oath to David—
       don't go back on your word:
    "I will set your offspring
       on your throne!
12 If your children keep my Covenant
       and my laws that I teach them,
    their descendants will sit
       on your throne forever."
13 For you chose Zion, Adonai;
       you wanted to live there:
14 "This is where I'll rest forever,
       it is here that I wanted to sit.
15 I will greatly bless its crops
       and I will fill its poor people with bread.
16 I will clothe its priests with salvation
       and make its faithful sing for joy.

¹⁷ Here David's stock will flower;
    I will light a lamp for my anointed one.
¹⁸ I will clothe his enemies with shame
    but the crown on his head will shine."

133

A Song of Ascents
By David

¹ See how good, how pleasant it is
    for God's people to live together as one!
² It is like precious oil on Aaron's head
    running down on his beard,
    running down to the collar of his robes.
³ It is like the dew of Mount Hermon,
    falling on the hills of Zion.
For that is where Our God bestows the blessing—
    life that never ends.

134

A Song of Ascents

¹ Come and bless Adonai,
    all you who serve Our God,
    ministering by night in God's house!
² Lift up your hands in the sanctuary,
    and bless Adonai!
³ May you be blessed from Zion
    by the One who made heaven and earth!

1 Alleluia!
  Praise the Name of Our God—
    sing praise, you who serve the Most High,
2 who stand in the house of Our God,
    in the courts of God's house!
3 Alleluia! God is good!
    Sing praise to that wonderful Name!
4 For you, Adonai, chose us for yourself,
    chose Israel as your treasure.

5 I know how great you are, Adonai,
    that you are above all gods.
6 Your will is done in heaven and on earth,
    in the seas and all their depths.
7 You summon clouds from the ends of the earth;
    you send lightning with the rain;
    you bring the wind from your storehouses.
8 You struck down all the firstborn of Egypt,
    human and beast alike.
9 You sent signs and wonders into Egypt's midst,
    against Pharaoh and all the royal attendants.
10 You struck down nations in their greatness
    and killed rulers in their splendor—
11 like Sihon, ruler of the Amorites,
    and Og, ruler of Bashan,
    and all the dominions of Canaan.
12 You gave their land, their inheritance, to Israel,
    an inheritance for your people.

13 Adonai, your Name stands forever,
    your fame is told from one generation to the next.
14 For you do justice for your people;
    and you have compassion for your faithful.
15 The idols of the nations are silver and gold,
    the work of human hands.
16 They have mouths but they can't speak;
    they have eyes but they can't see.
17 They have ears but can't hear;
    there is never a breath on their lips.

18 Their makers will come to be like them,
      and so will all who trust in them!

19 House of Israel, bless Our God!
      Priests of the Temple, bless Our God!
20 Attendants of the Sanctuary, bless Our God!
      You who revere Adonai, bless Our God!
21 Blessings from Zion upon Our God,
      who dwells in Jerusalem!
      Alleluia!

136

1 Thank you Adonai, for you are good!
        Your love is everlasting!
2 Thank you, God of gods!
        Your love is everlasting!
3 Thank you, Sovereign of sovereigns,
        Your love is everlasting!
4 you alone perform such great marvels.
        Your love is everlasting!
5 Your wisdom made the heavens.
        Your love is everlasting!
6 You spread the land out over the waters.
        Your love is everlasting!
7 You made the great lights:
        Your love is everlasting!
8 the sun to govern the day,
        Your love is everlasting!
9 moon and stars to govern the night.
        Your love is everlasting!
10 You struck down the firstborn of Egypt,
        Your love is everlasting!
11 and brought Israel out.
        Your love is everlasting!
12 With mighty hand and outstretched arm,
        Your love is everlasting!

13 you split the Sea of Reeds,
                    Your love is everlasting!
14 and led Israel through the middle,
                    Your love is everlasting!
15 and drowned Pharaoh and the armies of Egypt.
                    Your love is everlasting!
16 You led your people through the wilderness,
                    Your love is everlasting!
17 and struck down mighty rulers.
                    Your love is everlasting!
18 You cut down famous leaders,
                    Your love is everlasting!
19 like Sihon, ruler of the Amorites,
                    Your love is everlasting!
20 and Og, ruler of Bashan.
                    Your love is everlasting!
21 You gave their land as an inheritance,
                    Your love is everlasting!
22 an inheritance to Israel, your faithful one.
                    Your love is everlasting!
23 You remembered us when we were under the yoke,
                    Your love is everlasting!
24 and snatched us from our oppressors.
                    Your love is everlasting!

1 By the rivers of Babylon
   we sat and wept, remembering Zion.
2 On the willows there
   we hung up our harps.
3 For there our captors taunted us to sing our songs,
   our tormentors demanded songs of joy:
   "Sing us one of the songs of Zion!"
4 But how could we sing a song of Our God
   in a foreign land?

5 If I forget you, Jerusalem,
   may my right hand forget its skill!
6 May my tongue stick to the roof of my mouth
   if I ever forget you,
   if I ever stop considering Jerusalem
   my greatest joy.

7 Remember, Adonai, what the children of Edom did
   the day Jerusalem fell,
   when they said,
   "Tear it down!
   Tear it down to its foundations!"
8 Brood of Babylon, doomed to destruction,
   a blessing on those who will repay you
   for the evil you have done to us!
9 A blessing on those who will seize your infants
   and dash them against the rock!

1 I thank you with all my heart;
      I sing your praise before the gods.
2 I bow down in front of your holy Temple
      and praise your Name
   because of your love and faithfulness,
      for you have put above everything else
      your Name and your word.
3 When I called, you answered me—
      you made me bold and strong of heart.
4 All the rulers of the earth will praise you, Adonai,
      when they hear the words of your mouth.
5 They will sing about what you have done, Adonai,
      and about your great glory.
6 Even though you are so high above,
      you care for the lowly
      and see arrogant people from far away.
7 Even when I'm surrounded by troubles,
      you keep me safe;
   you oppose the anger of my enemies,
      and save me with your right hand.
8 You will do everything
      you have promised me.
   Adonai, your love is eternal;
      don't abandon the work of your hands.

For the conductor
A psalm of David

1 Adonai, you've searched me,
      and you know me.
2 You know if I am standing or sitting,
      you read my thoughts from far away.
3 Whether I walk or lie down, you are watching;
      you are intimate with all of my ways.
4 A word is not even on my tongue, Adonai,
      before you know what it is:
5 you hem me in, before and behind,
      shielding me with your hand.
6 Such knowledge is too wonderful for me,
      a height my mind cannot reach!

7 Where could I run from your Spirit?
      Where could I flee from your presence?
8 If I go up to the heavens, you're there;
      if I make my bed in Death, you're already there.
9 I could fly away with wings made of dawn,
      or make my home on the far side of the sea,
10 but even there your hand will guide me,
      your mighty hand holding me fast.
11 If I say, "The darkness will hide me,
      and night will be my only light,"
12 even darkness won't be dark to you;
      the night will shine like the day—
      darkness and light are the same to you.

13 You created my inmost being
      and stitched me together in my mother's womb.
14 For all these mysteries I thank you—
      for the wonder of myself,
   for the wonder of your works—
      my soul knows it well.
15 My frame was not hidden from you
      while I was being made in that secret place,
   knitted together in the depths of the earth;
16   your eyes saw my body even there.

All of my days
　　were written in your book,
all of them planned
　　before even the first of them came to be.
17 How precious your thoughts are to me, O God!
　　How impossible to number them!
18 I could no more count them
　　than I could count the sand.
But suppose I could?
　　You would still be with me!

19 O God, if only you would destroy those degenerates!
　　If only these reprobates would leave me alone!
20 They talk blasphemously about you;
　　your enemies treat you as if you were nothing.
21 Don't I hate those who hate you, Adonai?
　　Don't I loathe those who defy you?
22 I hate them with a total hatred,
　　and regard them as my own enemies!
23 Examine me, O God, and know my heart,
　　test me and know my thoughts—
24 see if there is misdeed within me,
　　and guide me in the way that is eternal.

For the conductor
A psalm of David

¹ Deliver me, Adonai, from these debased people;
    preserve me from the violent,
² who plan evil things in their hearts,
    and start new wars every day.
³ They make their tongue as forked as a snake's,
    their lips drip poison like a viper's.
⁴ Guard me, Adonai, from the hands of the bloodthirsty,
    —— *Selah* ——
    protect me from violent people,
    who deliberately try to trip me.
⁵ The arrogant lay their traps for me,
    and they've spread out the mesh of their net,
    they have set traps for me just off the path.
⁶ I say, "You are my God, Adonai!
    Hear my cries for mercy!"
⁷ Adonai, my Sovereign, my strong deliverer—
    you shield my head in the day of battle.
⁸ Adonai, don't fulfill the desires of the corrupt!
    Don't let their plans succeed,
    or their arrogance will be intolerable!
⁹ Let the trouble their lips have caused
    fall on their own heads!
¹⁰ Let burning coals fall upon them!
    Let them be tossed into the fire,
    or into a pit of quicksand, and never get out!
¹¹ Don't let a slanderer get a foothold in the land;
    let evil hunt down the violent and oppress *them*!

¹² I know that Our God makes sure the poor have justice,
    and defends those in need.
¹³ I know that those who love justice will praise your Name,
    and the upright will dwell in your presence.

A psalm of David

1   I call out to you, Adonai! Come quickly!
      Hear my voice when I call to you.
2   My prayers rise like incense before you,
        my hands rise to heaven like smoke from the evening sacrifice.
3   Adonai, set a guard at my mouth
        and keep watch at the gate of my lips—
4   don't let my heart be seduced by evil
          or by the lure of easy corruption in the company of evildoers!
        Don't let me sample their delights!
5   Let the upright strike me in reproof
        for my own good,
    but never let me allow the corrupt
        to anoint my head with oil!
        Daily I counter their malice with prayer.
6   When their leaders are flung off the edge of a cliff,
        they will learn how mild my words have been.
7   As a plow breaks up the earth,
        so our bones are scattered at the mouth of Sheol.
8   But to you, Adonai, I turn my eyes.
        I take shelter in you: don't abandon me to death!
9   Keep me from the traps that are set for me,
        from the bait laid for me by evildoers.
10 Let the violent fall into their own net,
        while I go on my way.

142

A teaching psalm
By David, when he was in the cave
A prayer

1 With all my voice, I cry to you, Adonai!
   With all my voice I cry for mercy!
2 I pour out my distress before you,
   I tell you all my troubles.
3 When my spirit faints within me,
   it is you who knows my way.
   On the path I walk
   they have hidden a snare to entrap me.
4 Look—there is no one beside me now,
   no one who stands with me.
   I have no place of refuge,
   no one to care about my life.
5 I cry to you, Adonai;
   I have said, "You are my refuge,
   all I have in the land of the living."
6 Listen, then, to my cry,
   for I am in the depths of despair.
   Rescue me from those who pursue me,
   for they are stronger than I.
7 Set me free from this prison
   so that your Name may be praised.
   The just will assemble around me
   because of your goodness to me.

1   Hear my prayer, Adonai,
      listen to my plea!
    In your faithfulness and justice
      answer me, give me relief!
2   Don't put your faithful one on trial,
      for no one who lives is innocent in your sight.
3   My enemy is pursuing me,
      grinding my life into the dirt.
    My enemy locks me in the deepest dungeon—
      I'm like those who died long ago.
4   I am totally dispirited,
      my heart is in deep despair.
5   I remember days gone by;
      I think about all you have done,
      and recall the works of your hands.
6   I lift up my hands to you in prayer;
      like dry ground, my soul thirsts for you!
                    —— *Selah* ——
7   Hurry up and answer me, Adonai!
      I'm ready to give up!
     Don't hide your face from me,
      or I'll be like those who go down to the Pit.
8   In the morning bring me word of your constant love,
      for I lift up my heart to you.
      Show me the path I should tread.
9   Rescue me from my enemies, Adonai,
      for you are my hiding place.
10 Teach me to do your will,
      for you are my God.
    Let your nurturing Spirit guide me
      on a safe and level path.
11 You keep me alive for the sake of your Name, Adonai;
      in your justice, rescue me from trouble.
12 In your love, you silence my enemies and destroy all my foes
      because I am loyal to you!

1 Blessed are you, Adonai, my rock,
    who trains my arms for battle,
    my hands for the struggle—
2 my refuge and my fortress, my stronghold,
    my deliverer, my shield, in whom I trust—
    who subdues entire nations under me.

3 Adonai, what are we,
    that you should care for us?
What is humankind,
    that you should think of us?
4 We are like a mist,
    our days like a passing shadow.

5 Part your skies, Adonai, and come down,
    touch the mountains, and they will smoke;
6 pitch your lightning bolts and put them to flight,
    shoot your arrows, and rout them!
7 Reach out your hand from on high—
    deliver me and rescue me from raging waters,
    from the hands of neighboring peoples
8 who make spurious promises and treaties
    while their right hands are raised in perjury.

9 O God, I'll sing a new song to you;
    with a ten-stringed lyre I'll sing your praise:
10 you are the source of the victory rulers claim,
    you delivered David, your faithful one, from the deadly sword.
11 Deliver me once again!
    Rescue me from the hands of neighboring peoples,
who make spurious promises and treaties
    while their right hands are raised in perjury.

12 Then our sons will be like plants,
    well-nurtured in their youth,
and our daughters like the strong pillars
    that stand at the corners of the palace.
13 Then our barns will be full,
    with every kind of provision;

our sheep will be in the thousands
    and the tens of thousands in our fields.
14 Our chieftains will be firmly established;
    there will be no exile, no cry of distress in the streets.
15 Happy are the people for whom this is true;
    happy are the people whose God is Adonai!

145*

A psalm of praise
By David

1   I will extol you, my God, my Ruler,
    and I will bless your Name forever and ever!
2   Every day will I bless you,
    and I will praise your Name forever and ever!
3   Great you are, Adonai, and greatly to be praised;
    your greatness is unfathomable.

4   Generation after generation praises your works
    and proclaims your mighty deeds,
5   they'll speak of the splendor of your glorious majesty,
    and I will meditate on your wondrous acts.
6   They'll discourse of the power of your awesome deeds,
    and I will declare your greatness.
7   They'll celebrate the fame of your abundant goodness,
    and I will joyfully sing of your justice.

8   Adonai, you are gracious and compassionate,
    slow to anger and rich in love.
9   Adonai, you are good to all
    and compassionate toward all your creatures.
10 All your creatures will praise you, Adonai,
    and your holy people will bless you.
11 They will tell of the glory of your reign
    and speak of your strength.

* This psalm is an acrostic poem: the first letter of each verse begins with a subsequent letter of the Hebrew alphabet.

12 You make known to all humankind your mighty acts
    and the glorious splendor of your reign.
13 Your reign is a reign for all the ages,
    and your dominion endures from generation to generation.

14 You lift up those who are falling
    and raise up those who are oppressed.
15 The eyes of all look to you in hope,
    and you give them their food in due season.
16 You open your hand
    and satisfy the desire of every living thing.
17 Adonai, you are just in all your ways
    and loving toward all that you have created.
18 You are near to all who call upon you,
    all who call upon you in truth.
19 You fulfill the desires of those who revere you;
    you hear their cry and save them.
20 You watch over all who love you, Adonai,
    but you'll destroy all who are corrupt.

21 My mouth will speak your praise, Adonai,
    and may all creation bless your holy Name
    forever and ever!

146

1 Alleluia!
    Praise Adonai, my soul!
2 I will praise you all my life;
    I will sing praise to my God while I live!

3 Do not trust in rulers,
    in mortals in whom there is no salvation.
4 When their spirits depart, they return to the earth,
    and on that day their plans perish.
5 Happy are those whose help is the God of Israel,
    whose hope is in Adonai, their God,

⁶ who made heaven and earth,
the sea and all that is in it!

Adonai, you keep faith forever:
⁷ you secure justice for the oppressed,
you give food to the hungry,
you set captives free,
⁸ you give sight to the blind,
you raise up those who were bowed down,
you love those who do justice,
⁹ you protect strangers,
you sustain orphans and the bereaved—
but you thwart the way of the corrupt.

¹⁰ Our God will reign forever—*your* God, Zion!—
through all generations. Alleluia!

147

¹ Alleluia!
How good it is to praise our God!
How pleasant and how fitting to sing God's praise!
² Our God rebuilds Jerusalem,
and gathers Israel's exiles.
³ God heals the brokenhearted,
and binds up their wounds.
⁴ God knows the number of the stars
and calls each one by name.
⁵ Great is Adonai, and mighty in power;
there is no limit to God's wisdom.
⁶ Our God lifts up the oppressed,
and casts the corrupt to the ground.

⁷ Sing to our God with thanksgiving,
sing praise with the harp to our God—
⁸ who covers the heavens with clouds,
who provides rain for the earth,

who makes grass sprout on the mountains
and herbs for the service of the people,*
9   who gives food to the cattle,
and to the young ravens when they cry.
10 God does not thrill to the strength of the horse,
or revel in the fleetness of humans.
11 Our God delights in those who worship with reverence
and put their hope in divine love.

12 Jerusalem, give glory to Adonai!
Zion, praise your God!
13 For God strengthens the bars of your gates,
and blesses your children within you.
14 God has granted peace within your borders,
and fills you with the finest wheat.

15 God sends forth a command to the earth—
swiftly runs the word!
16 God spreads snow like wool
and scatters frost like ashes.
17 God hurls hail like pebbles—
who can stand before God's freezing winds?
18 Then God sends a word and melts them;
God lets the breeze blow and the waters run again.

19 God's words have been revealed to the chosen people,
God's decrees and laws to Israel.
20 God has not done this with any other nation;
They do not know God's law.
Alleluia!

---

* This verse is found in the Greek version of the text, but is missing from the standard Hebrew version.

1 Alleluia!
  Praise Our God from the heavens,
    praise God in the heights!
2 Praise God, all you angels,
    praise God, all you hosts!
3 Praise God, sun and moon,
    praise God, all you shining stars!
4 Praise God, you highest heavens,
    and you waters above the heavens!
5 Let them praise the Name of Our God,
    by whose command they were created.
6 God established them forever and ever
    and gave a decree which won't pass away.
7 Praise Our God from the earth,
    you sea creatures and ocean depths,
8 lightning and hail, snow and mist,
    and storm winds that fulfill God's word,
9 mountains and all hills,
    fruit trees and all cedars,
10 wild animals and all cattle,
    small animals and flying birds,
11 rulers of the earth, leaders of all nations,
    all the judges in the world,
12 young men and young women,
    old people and children—
13 let them all praise the Name of Our God
    whose Name alone is exalted,
14 whose majesty transcends heaven and earth,
    and who has raised up a Horn for God's people
  to the praise of the faithful,
    the children of Israel, the people dear to God!
  Alleluia!

1 Alleluia!
   Sing to Our God a new song!
   Sing praise in the assembly of the faithful.
2 Let Israel be glad in its Maker,
   let the children of Zion rejoice in their God.
3 Let them praise God's Name
   with festive dance,
let them sing praise
   with timbrel and harp.
4 For Our God loves the people,
   and crowns the lowly with salvation.
5 Let the faithful exult in this honor,
   let them sing for joy in their beds—
6 let the high praise of God be in their throats.
And let two-edged swords be in their hands
7 to execute vengeance on the nations
   and punishment on the peoples,
8 to bind their rulers with chains
   and their nobles with fetters of iron,
9 to carry out their sentence to the letter.
   This is the glory of all the faithful.
Alleluia!

1   Alleluia!
    We praise you, Adonai, in your sanctuary,
       we praise you in your mighty skies!
2   We praise you for your powerful deeds,
       we praise you for your overwhelming glory!
3   We praise you with the blast of the trumpet,
       we praise you with lyre and harp!
4   We praise you with timbrel and dance,
       we praise you with strings and flute!
5   We praise you with clashing cymbals,
       we praise you with resounding cymbals!
6   Let everything that has breath
       praise Our God!
    Alleluia!

appendix:

pronunciation guide

a

Abba	**AH**-buh	Amelek	**AHM**-eh-leck
Abimelech	ah-**BIM**-eh-leck	Ammon	**AH**-mon
Abiram	ah-**BEER**-ahm	Amorites	**AM**-or-ites
Absalom	**AHB**-sah-lom	Arameans	ah-**RAHM**-e-ans
Adonai	ah-doe-**NYE**	Asaph	**AY**-saff
Ahimelech	ah-**HIM**-eh-leck	Assyria	a-**SEER**-ee-ah
Aleph	**AH**-leff	Ayin	**EYE**-in

b

Baal of Peor	buh-**ALL** of pay-**OR**	Babylon	**BAB**-ih-lon
Bashan	Buh-**SHAHN**	Beth	**BAYT**
Bathsheba	Bath-**SHE**-buh	Byblos	**BEE**-blose

c

Canaan	**KAY**-nan	Cush	(rhymes with **push**)
Cassia	**KASS**-ee-ah		

∂

Daleth .... **DAH**-let

Dathan .... dah-**THAHN**

Doeg .... **DOE**-egg

e

Edom .... **EE**-dom

Edomites .... **EE**-doe-mites

Endor .... **EN**-dor

Ephraim .... eh-fry-**EEM**

Ephraimite .... **EH**-fry-eem-ite

Ephrata .... eh-**FRA**-tah

Ethan .... **EE**-than

Ethiopia .... eeth-ee-**OH**-pee-ah

Euphrates .... yew-**FRAY**-tees

Ezraite .... **EZ**-rah-ite

f

Fakir .... fah-**KEER**

g

Gath .... **GATH**

Ghimel .... **GIH**-mel

Gilead .... **GIL**-ee-ad

Gittite .... **GIT**-ite

h

Hagar .... **HAY**-gar

He .... **HAY**

Heman .... **HAY**-man

Hermon .... **HER**-mon

Heth .... **HET**

Horeb .... **HOR**-eb

Hyssop .... **HISS**-op

i

Ishmaelites .... **ISH**-may-el-ites

j

Jabin .... jah-**BEEN**

Jeduthun .... **JED**-oo-thun

Joab .... **JOE**-ab

Judah .... **JU**-dah

k

Kadesh .... **KAH**-desh

Kaph .... **KAHF**

Kedar .... **KAY**-dar

Kishon .... kih-**SHON**

l

Lamed .... **LAH**-med

Lebanon .... **LEH**-ba-non

Leviathan .... leh-**VYE**-a-than

Manasseh	mah-**NASS**-ah	Mesech	**MAY**-sekh
Massah	**MASS**-ah	Midian	**MIH**-dee-an
Melchizedek	mel-**KIZ**-eh-dek	Mizar	**MYE**-zar
Mem	**MEM**	Moab	**MOE**-ab
Meribah	**MARE**-ih-bah		

Naphtali	naf-**TAL**-ee	Nun	**NOON**
Nathan	**NAY**-than		

Og	**OH**g	Oreb	**OR**-eb
Ophir	oh-**FEER**		

Pe	**PAY**	Philistines	**FILL**-iss-tynes
Peor, Baal of	pay-**OR**, buh-**ALL** of	Phinehas	**FIN**-ee-as
Philistia	fill-**ISS**-tee-ah		

Qoph	**KOFE**	Qorach	**KOR**-ackh

Rahab	**RAY**-hab	Resh	**RAYSH**

Sabaoth	sah-bah-**OAT**	Shiloh	**SHY**-lo
Salem	**SAY**-lem	Shin	**SHIN**
Samekh	**SAH**-mek	Shofar	**SHOW**-far
Sechem	**SEKH**-em	Sihon	see-**HONE**
Selah	**SAY**-lah	Sinai	**SYE**-nye
Shaddai	shah-**DYE**	Sirion	**SEER**-ee-on
Sheol	**SHAY**-ole	Sisera	**SIS**-er-a

Tabor	**TAY**-bor	Tsadhe	**TZAD**-deh
Tarshish	**TAR**-shish	Tyre	**TIRE**
Taw	**TAW**	Tyrian	**TEER**-ee-an
Teth	**TET**		

pronunciation guide

Waw .... **WAW**

Yearim .... yay-ar-**EEM**   Yod .... **YOOD** (rhymes with **should**)

Zalmon .... **ZAHL**-mon   Zebah .... **ZAY**-bah
Zalmunna .... zahl-**MOON**-ah   Zeeb .... **ZAY**-eb
Zalu .... **ZAH**-loo

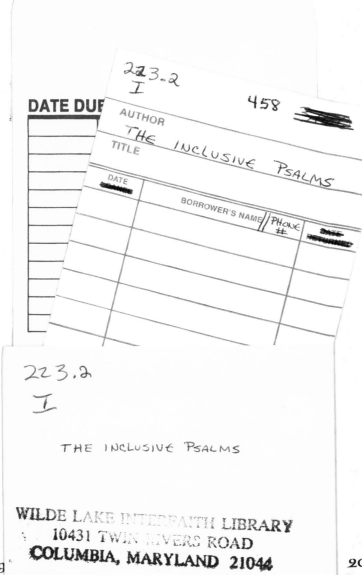